Coastal Walks
around Anglesey

The coastal path near Rhoscolyn

Coastal Walks around Anglesey

Carl Rogers

Mara Publications

First published in May 1996 by **Mara Publications**,
22 Crosland Terrace, Helsby, Cheshire WA6 9LY

All enquiries regarding sales, telephone: (01928) 723744

ISBN 0 9522409 6 3

Acknowledgements

I would like to say a special thank you to the following individuals for their help in preparing this book: Jack Rogers for taking two of the photographs and checking all the routes along with Audrey Rogers, David Telfer and Martin Ogden; Chris Mitchell for his "tireless dedication" (to use his words) in proofing the text to such a tight deadline and Chris Davies for use of the aerial photograph on page 94.

Cover photographs: *front - the northern coast near Cemaes Bay (walk 7)*
rear - looking south from Ynys Llanddwyn (walk 14)

Layout and design by Mara Publications.
Text, maps and photographs © Carl Rogers 1995

British Library Cataloguing-in-publication data.
A catalogue is available for this book from the British Library.

Sketch maps based on the Ordnance Survey 1:25 000 map with the permission of the Controller of HM Stationary Office.

Printed and bound by MFP Design & Print, telephone 0161-864 4540

Contents

Introduction

Anglesey lies off the North Wales coast separated from the mainland by the Menai Strait; a long arm of the sea less than 300 yards wide at Menai Bridge and a little under a mile wide at Caernarfon. Although physically separated from the mainland, geologically it is part of the coastal plain which stretches north and west from the mountains of Snowdonia. The Pre-Cambrian rocks of its foundation are very old with overlays of younger shale, visible at Parys Mountain and limestone, which can be seen on the east of the island around Penmon and Llanddona. On top of this there is a thick covering of boulder clay and glacial drift, giving the island its rich fertile soil, making it what it is today and has been since the Middle Ages - farming country.

The occasional visitor en-route to the ferry terminal at Holyhead, whose only view of the island is the 20 miles of dull undulating farmland seen from the A5, could be forgiven for thinking that Anglesey has little to offer. Especially in poor weather does this landscape seem to epitomise all that is depressing about Wales. The reason for this is its underlying structure - a series of flat low-lying valleys running across the island from northeast to southwest. In fact there are few points within its 290 square miles that rise above 400 feet. Where this does happen however, such as at Mynydd Bodafon (route 4) and Holyhead Mountain (route 11), the views are extensive.

Thankfully, unlike the interior, the coast is anything but dull and unchanging; in fact Anglesey can boast some of the finest and most varied coastal scenery in Britain. The uniform plan of the island, looking a little like the letter 'Q' tipped on its side, does not seem to have created a lack of detailed interest around the coast. There are wide tidal estuaries, sandy bays separated by rocky headlands and dramatic cliff scenery sheltering quiet coves.

For the walker, there is good access to this ever changing coastline and for much of its length there is a well maintained coastal footpath. This is complemented inland by a vast network of public rights of way, although it has to be said that at the time of writing these are not always in good repair, especially in the less frequented areas.

Climatically, the island has much to recommend it, being one of the driest and mildest parts of North Wales. Often, you will be able to enjoy hours of warm sunshine here, while the highland areas of Snowdonia lie draped in mist and rain just a few miles away.

This close proximity to the mountains gives the island another big advantage over coastal areas elsewhere. Except on parts of the northern coast, the mountains provide an ever-

South Stack, Holy Island

Looking towards the hills of Lleyn from Ynys Llanddwyn

present backdrop to intricate coastal foregrounds. This interplay of coast and mountain produce such unrivalled views as that of the Lleyn Peninsula and its shapely hills from the beach at Aberffraw (route 13) and Ynys Llanddwyn (route 14).

In addition, there is a rich historic heritage with visible remains of settlement reaching back into the second millennium BC. In fact Anglesey has one of the highest concentrations of prehistoric sites in Britain.

The position of Anglesey, thrust out into the Irish Sea, along with its gentle terrain and rich fertile soil of the interior, have ensured that it has been populated from the earliest times. In the 1,500 years before the Romans conquered Britain, various tribes settled in these islands and their method of travel, both for exploration and trade, seems to have been primarily by sea. As such, Anglesey was ideally placed at a crucial point in the seaways of western Britain. Unfortunately, this has also made it vulnerable to attack and invasion, which became a major feature of its early history.

The fact that Anglesey was densely populated in prehistoric times is made evident by large numbers of megalithic tombs, which represent the earliest visible remains of settlement on the island. Fine examples can be seen in fields near Traeth Lligwy (route 3) and Brynsiencyn (route 15). Visitors to the restored burial chamber known as Bryn Celli Ddu near Llanddaniel Fab, can see the original form of these monuments.

The next phase of settlement, known as the Bronze Age, brought immigrants known as the 'Beaker' people to Anglesey toward the end of the second millennium BC. It was these tribes who raised the island's many standing stones, although their purpose remains a mystery.

Many speculate on a possible religious significance and this could well be the case, for by the fifth century BC, Celtic tribes had begun to move into Britain and by the time of the Roman conquest, Anglesey had become the most important centre for the Celtic or 'old religion' in Europe. The writings of Julius Caesar suggest that the Druid religion was developed in Britain and exported to other Celtic tribes in Northern Europe. If this is true, the Celts may well have developed what was already being practised here when they arrived.

This religion was taught by a class of priests or 'Druids' and it seems to have been they who stirred up the greatest resistance to the Roman occupation of Britain. There seems little doubt that it was to stamp out this seat of spiritual resistance, that the Roman leader Suetonius Paulinus set out to invade Anglesey in AD 61. With an army of over 10,000 he crossed the Menai Strait and in one easily won battle extinguished the old Celtic religion completely. The sacred groves were destroyed and the Druid priesthood wiped out.

The fact that so little is now known about this religion and indeed about much of the early history of the Celts is due to the fact that they committed nothing to writing; all their religious teaching and history was passed on orally. All manner of fanciful and gruesome practices have been attributed to the Druids but nothing is really known about them for sure. Their knowledge and traditions died with them on the shores of the Menai Strait almost 2,000 years ago.

It was the Celts who introduced the Iron Age culture to Britain and are perhaps best known today for the many hill forts which can be seen all over the country. Anglesey is no exception and a number are visible today, with fine examples at Holyhead Mountain (route 11) and Bwrdd Arthur (route 2). Perhaps the most impressive remains from this period are to be found at Din Lligwy near Moelfre (route 3). Here the visitor needs little imagination to visualise the settlement as it was; hut bases, doorways and enclosure walls are all clearly visible.

The Roman occupation left surprisingly few remains on Anglesey, which was probably controlled from the fort at Caernarfon (Segontium). The most notable are to be found at Holyhead, where the walls of a coastal fort still enclose the church and the base of a lookout tower known as Caer y Twr, stands inside the old hill fort on Holyhead Mountain (route 11).

If you stand on this summit today, you will get a fine view out to sea in all directions, but on a clear evening you will see out to the west the Wicklow Mountains of southern Ireland and it was from here, when the protective arm of Rome

The well preserved remains of Din Lligwy

had been removed, that raiders came in the early post-Roman era. These invasions inevitably resulted in settlement and it may be significant that the hut circles on Holyhead Mountain (route 11) are known today as 'Cytiau'r Gwyddelod' or the 'Irishmen's Huts'.

The Irish invasion became such a problem to the inhabitants, not only of Anglesey but also the whole of North Wales, that a powerful Celtic chieftain came down from Strathclyde and devoted the rest of his life to ridding the land of these

11

invaders. His name was Cunedda and it was in a last battle on Anglesey that the Irish were finally defeated and expelled from Wales in about AD 470.

Cunedda established himself at Aberffraw where he built a palace close to the site of the present day village (route 13). In doing so, he founded a dynasty which would rule North Wales for almost eight centuries and produce such great rulers as Rhodri Mawr, Gruffydd ap Cynan, Owain Gwynedd, Llywelyn the Great and his grandson Llywelyn the Last, whose defeat by Edward I in 1282 brought a final end to Welsh independence.

The reign of Maelgwyn Gwynedd, a descendant of Cunedda's, saw the firm establishment of Christianity in Anglesey, with the founding of monasteries at Penmon (route 1) and Holyhead by Saint Seiriol and Saint Cybi. Although he is said to have been a wicked ruler, the land on which these monasteries were built was granted by Maelgwyn. Perhaps he was looking for divine favour towards the end of his life.

The rule of the Welsh princes is unfortunately a rather sad period, being marked more by treachery than any great advancement. The progress made by some of its greatest rulers was often destroyed by the infighting of their descendants. This was caused in part by the tradition of dividing a man's possessions equally between his sons following his death. This meant that at best his kingdom was much weakened, particularly if he had many sons which was often the case. Thus, brothers frequently fought each other for their share of the kingdom and rivals were often eliminated or imprisoned. Others made alliances with former enemies outside Wales in a desperate bid to gain what they saw as their birthright.

These divisions were quickly exploited by Saxons and Normans from across the English border. It also meant that when threatened, Wales was never able to defend itself with a united force.

During the early years of the ninth century a new menace presented itself; one that came to be feared throughout the British Isles and one that Anglesey was particularly vulnerable to: Viking raids. By this time the Vikings had formed colonies at Dublin and in the Isle of Man and from there they launched attacks all along the Welsh coast. The monasteries at Holyhead and Penmon were attacked in 961 and 971 and the palace at Aberffraw was partially destroyed in 968. The Vikings left no settlements on Anglesey but a number of names remain as evidence of their passing; notably Priestholm (Puffin Island) and the Skerries off the northwestern tip of Anglesey (route 9).

Penmon Priory

The Norman conquest had little impact on Anglesey initially, although an early raid by the Earl of Chester in 1090 led to the building of a motte and bailey castle at Aberlleiniog (route 1) near Beaumaris. This was soon destroyed by the powerful Gruffydd ap Cynan and the Normans made little real progress against the Welsh for the next 100 years.

When the threat of Viking raids ceased towards the end of the eleventh century, a period of prosperity followed and with an increase in population, a programme of church building began. This was the first time churches had been built in stone and a number have survived in part from this period, notably Hen Chapel near Din Lligwy (route 3).

It was also during this time that deforestation of the interior of the island was finally achieved, releasing rich fertile

Beaumaris Castle

land for agriculture and earning Anglesey the name 'Mon, Mam Cymru'- *Anglesey, Mother of Wales*. This referred to the vast quantities of grain which were grown here during the Middle Ages, sufficient it is said for the whole of Wales.

During the wars of Llywelyn the Great and his grandson Llywelyn the Last, the importance of Anglesey's ability to feed Wales was realised and both King John and Edward I made attempts to take Anglesey, thus depriving Wales of its food supply. It was the loss of Anglesey which finally brought Llywelyn the Great out of hiding in the highlands of Snowdonia to bargain with King John and ensured Edward's victory against Llywelyn the Last in 1282.

Following his conquest of Wales, Edward embarked on a programme of castle building all along the North Wales coast, the ruins of which still stand. On Anglesey he built his last Welsh castle at Beaumaris in 1295 near the site of Llywelyn's court.

Wales was now subject to the English crown and the title 'Prince of Wales' reserved for the king's eldest son. The wars of independence were over, although Owain Glyndwr was to raise the Welsh banner briefly at the beginning of the fifteenth century.

Although Wales was never to see independence from the English crown again, it did produce one of the most influential ruling families ever to sit on the throne of England - the Tudors. The seat of this family was Plas Penmynydd here in Anglesey and Henry Tudor's claim to the throne came through his descent from Owain Tudor and his rather mysterious marriage in 1429 to Henry V's widow, Queen Catherine.

The late sixteenth century saw an increased demand for copper, required for the production of cannons and a host of household items. The Tudors were instrumental in restricting the import of foreign metal and the subsequent rise in

15

the price of copper created a boom towards the end of the seventeenth century. The abandoned mines at Parys Mountain and the development of Amlwch as a port, are the result of the discovery and exploitation of one of the richest deposits of copper in the country.

The heyday of the industry was between 1760 and 1815 and the higher wages offered by the mining company took many workers off the land during these years. Another industry from this period which we can still see remains of today, is that of milling and a number of old windmill towers still stand as testimony to Anglesey's former corn production.

Anglesey's position in the Liverpool sea lane and its proximity to Ireland have produced a rich maritime history. By the seventeenth century, packet boats were regularly crossing to Ireland, providing a service which was to expand in the nineteenth century when Thomas Telford completed his London to Holyhead coach road (A5) and built the graceful suspension bridge over the Menai Strait in 1826.

Anglesey's rocky, treacherous coastline presented a constant hazard to shipping and there were literally hundreds of shipwrecks during the nineteenth century alone. The most famous wreck was that of the *Royal Charter*, which hit rocks and sank off Moelfre (route 3) in 1859 with the loss of over 400 lives. The lighthouses which dot the coast today date mainly from this period although they are now all automated.

Today, tourism plays a key role in the island's economy and with recent road improvements on the mainland cutting the travelling time from Merseyside and Greater Manchester, Anglesey has become a popular venue for weekend breaks and second holidays. Away from the coast however, agriculture still dominates, although the emphasis is now on cattle and dairy farming, with little or no sign of its once famous corn fields.

Maps

Although this book contains all the information needed to follow the walks, it is recommended that you obtain copies of the relevant Ordnance Survey maps. Two series are of interest to the walker: the Pathfinder and Landranger series.

The Pathfinder maps are very detailed and are excellent for exploration showing all field boundaries, woods, buildings and also carry public rights of way information. The Landranger series is less detailed but ideal for locating the start of each walk and identifying additional features along the way. If you only buy one map to use with this book, this should be your choice; one sheet covers the whole island.

Landranger Series: sheet 114 Anglesey.

Pathfinder Series: sheets 733, 734, 735, 750, 751, 752 and 768.

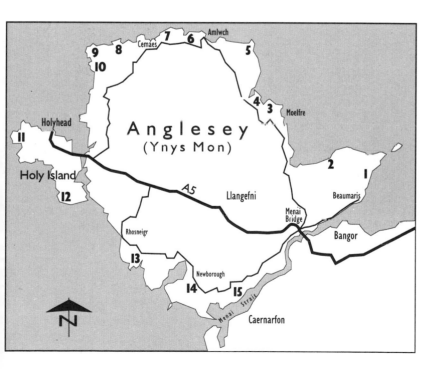

Glossary of Welsh names

Aber	*river mouth*	Dyffryn	*valley*
Abaty	*abbey*	Eglwys	*church*
Afon	*river*	Eryri	*highland*
Bach	*little*	Esgair	*ridge*
Bryn	*eminence*	Fach	*small*
Cae	*field, enclosure*	Faes	*meadow*
Caer	*fort*	Fawr	*large*
Canol	*middle*	Felin	*mill*
Capel	*chapel*	Ffordd	*road*
Carn, Carnedd	*heap of stones*	Ffynnon	*well or fountain*
Carreg	*crag or stone*	Foel	*bare hill*
Castell	*castle or fortress*	Gaer	*camp*
Cefn	*ridge*	Galt	*slope*
Clogwyn	*cliff*	Garn	*an eminence*
Clwyd	*gate*	Glas	*blue-green*
Coch	*red*	Glyn	*deep valley*
Coed	*wood*	Goch	*red*
Cors	*bog or swamp*	Gors	*swamp*
Craig	*crag*	Grach	*scabby*
Crib	*jagged ridge*	Groes	*cross*
Croes	*cross*	Gwern	*alder coppice*
Cwm	*coombe*	Gwyn	*white*
Dinas	*natural fortress*	Hafod	*summer dwelling*
Ddu	*black*	Hen	*old*

Isaf	*lower*	Rhyd	*ford*
Llan	*church*	Sarn	*causeway*
Llyn	*lake*	Tomen	*mound*
Llys	*hall or court*	Traeth	*beach, sandy shore*
Lon	*lane*	Tref	*town*
Maen	*stone*	Trwyn	*peninsula*
Maes	*field or meadow*	Twll	*cavern*
Mawr	*large*	Twr	*tower*
Moel	*rounded hill*	Ty	*house*
Mor	*sea*	Tyddyn	*farmstead*
Morfa	*flat seashore, sea fen*	Uchaf	*upper*
Mynach	*monk*	Waun	*moorland*
Mynydd	*mountain*	Wen	*white*
Newydd	*new*	Wern	*alder swamp*
Ogof	*cave*	Y, Yr	*the*
Pant	*hollow*	Yn	*in*
Parc	*park*	Ynys	*island*
Pen	*point*		
Penrhyn	*promontory*		
Pentre	*village*		
Pistyll	*waterfall*		
Plas	*house*		
Pont	*bridge*		
Porth	*port*		
Pwll	*pool*		

 Penmon

Distance: *6½ miles*

Start: There is a small car park in the village of Llangoed. This is situated on the right, at the northern end of the village, just before the little bridge over Afon Lleiniog. *Grid ref. 611 797 (Landranger 114, Pathfinder 752).*

The Route

1. Turn right out of the car park, cross the little bridge and turn right again almost immediately onto an access road. Where this forks after a few yards, keep right and follow a concrete road for some distance to a water treatment works on the left. Bear right here onto a woodland path with a stream to your left and continue to the road.

Part way along the path you will see the ruins of Castell Aberlleiniog hidden among the trees on your left. This is the site of a Norman motte and bailey castle built by Hugh de Avranches, Earl of Chester in 1090. It stood on a mound which is still almost 30 feet high and over 150 feet wide and would originally have been built of timber. The present ruins date from the late medieval period.

This first advance into Anglesey by the Normans was short lived, the powerful Gruffydd ap Cynan captured and destroyed the castle just three years later. After this setback, Anglesey was abandoned by the Normans for over 100 years.

Turn left now and walk along the lane. The lane bends left just before the shore and there is a car park on the right; just beyond this and immediately after a house on the right ("Cerrig"), a path between gardens on the right leads down onto a shingle beach.

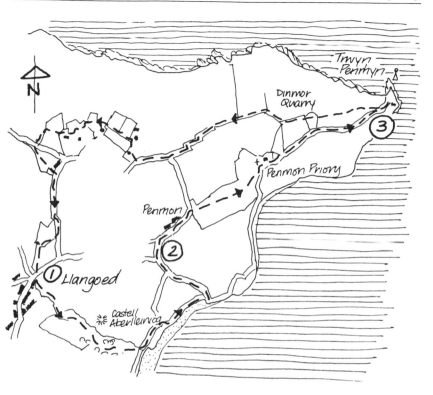

If the tide allows, turn left and walk along the shore to the concrete ramp at the end of the small bay. Turn left here and follow the lane to the first distinct left-hand bend. (Alternatively, if the tide does not allow, reach this point by continuing along the lane). Continue straight ahead here (or turn left if you did not walk along the beach) and at a left-hand bend go straight ahead on a rising access road between cottages.

2. At the top of the rise, turn right along the lane and walk through the tiny hamlet of Penmon. As the lane bears left beyond the houses, look for a signed footpath on the right which enters fields by means of stone steps and an iron gate in the wall.

21

The right of way takes a direct line through a large field with the Great Orme directly ahead. Lower down the field, the ruins of Penmon Priory and dovecote come into view. Bear half-left now and follow a faint track which leads to a large metal gate which is often locked. Do not go through the gate, turn left instead and look for stone steps and a gate on the right just before the priory buildings. Go through the gate and turn left along the road.

The existing priory buildings date from the latter half of the twelfth century and housed a community of Augustinian monks until the Dissolution, when the lands were granted to the Bulkeley family. The site is traditionally associated with the monastery of Saint Seiriol, the sixth century friend of Saint Cybi who lived on Holy Island.

A popular story concerning these two friends relates how once a week they each walked half way across the island to meet at a well near Llanerchymedd. The walk to and from this central meeting place meant that Cybi had the sun in his face both morning and evening and became known as Cybi the Dark; while Seiriol always had the sun at his back and became know as Seiriol the Fair.

Seiriol was a descendant of Cunedda, a powerful chieftain who expelled Irish invaders from Anglesey during the fifth century and a second cousin of King Maelgwyn Gwynedd. The land on which he built his church at Penmon is said to have been granted by his royal cousin. Today, little or nothing from Seiriol's time has survived although the hut circle adjacent to Saint Seiriol's Well is reputed to be the remains of his cell.

The Celtic monastery that Seiriol established here suffered badly in the late tenth century when there were repeated attacks from Viking raiders all along this coast. Two carved stone crosses from this period can be seen inside the church.

After the Dissolution of the Monasteries in the sixteenth century, the land and buildings passed into the ownership of the

Bulkeley family who established the deer park and built the dovecote about 1600. This impressive little building was built by Richard Bulkeley to house over 1,000 birds and would have provided an important source of fresh meat. Eggs would have been collected by means of a ladder supported on the central stone pillar which stands over twelve feet high.

Follow the toll road down to the end of the headland at Trwyn-du or Penmon Point (no fee for those on foot).

At the end of the road there is a small cafe and toilets which are open during the summer season. Just offshore, a tall black and white automatic lighthouse warns shipping of the dangerous sound between Anglesey's most easterly headland and Puffin Island.

The lighthouse at Penmon Point

This tiny island has at least three names, each telling us something of its history or character. In Welsh it is known as "Ynys Seiriol", after the sixth century saint who founded the monastic settlement at Penmon and built a second monastery on the island. In the following century Cadwallon, King of Gwynedd, was besieged here by Edwin, the Saxon king of Northumbria, during a time of Saxon expansion into Wales.

The ruins which can be seen today are the remains of a twelfth century church which replaced earlier buildings once the threat of Viking raids had ceased. This brings us to the island's second name: "Priestholm" which is Norse in origin. The name undoubtedly refers to the monastic community which thrived when the Vikings first came here in the tenth century.

The only other building on the island is a small nineteenth century semaphore station, part of a chain which extended all along the coast from Holyhead to Liverpool. Messages were transmitted visually by means of signs supported on masts and movable arms. Though rather crude by modern standards, it proved to be amazingly effective in its day and could transmit a message from Holyhead to Liverpool in just a few minutes. The island's only inhabitants today are sea birds, among them puffins from which it gets its most recent English name: "Puffin Island".

3. Walk back to the little cafe and bear half-right across the grass. A narrow, though well worn and waymarked footpath cuts through the bracken from here. Ignore other paths to the right and left until a large ladder stile leads over the wall into grazing fields. Take a direct line through the first field and turn right along a track which leads into Dinmor Park Quarry. Immediately before the quarry entrance, turn left over a stile and walk through a large field keeping right beside the wall. In the field corner bear right through the gate and again keep beside the old deer park wall on your left.

Bear left over a stile at the head of the field and again stay beside the wall passing an old hut circle about half way along the wall. Enter a narrow lane beside a small white cottage on the right and walk along the lane for about 600 yards to the first junction. Go straight ahead here and after about 300 yards turn right down the drive to a number of houses. Just before the garden of the last house turn left through an iron kissing gate onto an enclosed footpath which shortly leads into fields. Keep to the left-hand field edge in three small fields and pass through a kissing gate beside a cottage. Turn left for a few yards and then right through a second gate adjacent to the cottage. Bear half-left now and look for an iron gate in the far hedge (ignore a faint track to the right).

Keep left in the following field and join an access track beside a small cottage. After a short rise, bear right following a signed footpath through an area of gorse. Just before a large gate leads into fields, turn left through an iron kissing gate and keep right along the edge of a large garden. At the end of the garden bear right through a second kissing gate and follow an enclosed footpath with a high wall to the right. At the end of the path turn right down a short drive to a lane.

Bear half-right here to where an iron kissing gate leads into fields again. Keep to the field edge and in the bottom left-hand corner of the field, stone steps lead over the wall onto a track. Turn left along the track keeping left at a fork. A large gate leads into a quiet lane and a kissing gate opposite continues the right of way. Bear to the left now, following a faint track in the direction of the church, to join the lane beside the cemetery. Turn right down the lane passing the school and look for a signed footpath on the right after about 600 yards. Keep to the field edge and at the bottom of the field turn left over a footbridge, passing a small cottage on the right. Walk down the drive to the road and turn right returning to point 1.

2. Llanddona

Distance: *6 miles*

Start: Drive into Llanddona from the south and bear right by the Owen Glyndwr public house. Just after the road turns sharp left on the edge of the village, bear right again and park on the verge just before the lane forks.
Grid ref. 579 795 (Landranger 114, Pathfinder 751 & 753).

The Route

1. Keep right at the fork and continue down the lane to Llaniestyn church on the left.

To the right there is a fine view over the rolling green fields of eastern Anglesey which contrast so sharply with the barren, windswept west. Beyond lie the rugged heights of Snowdonia.

Turn left down the track to the church and look for a stile to the right of the little cemetery which leads into fields. Bear half-left in the first field aiming to the right of a small farm where a ladder stile leads over the wall. Walk through a smaller field now aiming for an old iron kissing gate in the far hedge. In the third field keep to the right-hand field edge and enter a narrow lane with "Tyddyn Uchaf" farm to your right.

Turn right and walk along the lane for about ½ mile. Immediately before the first farmhouse on the left ("Cefn") turn left over a stile beside a large gate and follow a green lane which shortly leads into fields. Keep to field edges now with the hedge to your right initially then, after a new metal kissing gate, keep the hedge to your left passing a large farmhouse also on the left. Immediately beyond the farm turn left through a gate, then after a few yards turn left through a

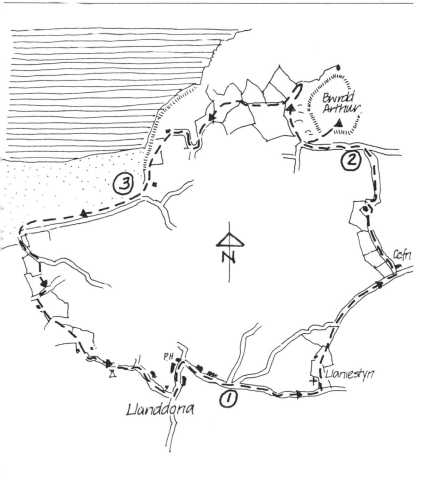

second gate to join a track at the back of the house. Turn right now and follow the track to the road.

2. Turn left along the road and look for a signed footpath on the right after about 500 yards. Almost immediately a faint path rises on the right to the summit of Bwrdd Arthur. It must be noted that this is not a public right of way although it is extensively walked and there appears to be no problem with its use.

Walking along the beach, Red Wharf Bay

This impressive limestone plateau forms a natural fortress and supported a British settlement similar to Din Lligwy near Moelfre (walk 3) during the Iron Age and early Roman period. Today, the remains, though far less impressive than Din Lligwy, can still be identified and include a defence wall (originally 5-8 feet thick) enclosing a site of almost 17 acres along with several hut circles. Finds date mainly from the Roman period.

In clear weather you can enjoy uninterrupted views in all directions with features as far away as the Isle of Man, the fells of the Lake District and the Lancashire coast visible across the Irish Sea to the north. Eastwards, the limestone headland of the Great Orme stands beyond Puffin Island, with the lighthouse at Penmon marking Anglesey's eastern-most point.

To the south, the high rounded tops of the Carneddau rise behind the towns of Penmaenmawr and Llanfairfechan with the serrated outline of Snowdon farther west. In the far distance, the triple peaks of Yr Eifl (The Rivals) form a backdrop to the cultivated landscape of eastern Anglesey. Westwards, the wooded slopes of Mynydd Llwydiarth fall to the wide sweep of Red Wharf Bay with Benllech, Moelfre and Mynydd Bodafon beyond.

Return to the stile at the foot of the hill and turn right onto a contouring footpath through the gorse with a wide view of the bay immediately ahead.

Follow the path until it begins to curve around the hillside and just before farm buildings turn sharp left onto a rough track which shortly runs into fields beyond a gate. Turn right and keep to the field edge in the next two fields. In the right-hand corner of the second field, a well hidden stile leads onto National Trust land at Bryn Offa. Descend a gorse and heather-clad slope to join a track and turn left.

Follow the track to a T junction, turn right and keep right again at a fork. At the end of the track there is a white cottage and a field gate on the left immediately in front. Go through the gate and bear half-right down the slope to a stile, continuing down the slope to an old kissing gate on the edge of the crumbling sea cliffs. Walk along the edge of the cliffs until your way is blocked by the garden of a cottage adjacent to the beach. Reach the beach by keeping to the right of the garden although the path is quite overgrown. At the time of writing steps are being taken to improve the right of way.

3. Turn left along the beach. As you walk along the sand, a number of paths lead off to the left to join a sandy track which runs parallel to the beach. Take one of these paths and turn right along the track. After a left-hand bend continue for about 250 yards and look for a grassy track which runs through a field on the right (no sign). Follow the track across two small fields to a gate. Beyond the gate, rise to a T junction with a more defined track and turn right. After about 100 yards turn left through an iron kissing gate and approach a small white-washed farmhouse. Go through the gate and pass in front of the house to join a path which bears diagonally-left up the bracken covered bank. This section of the route may be quite overgrown late in the summer, although when the route was walked the path was well maintained. If you do encounter any problems on this stretch, return to the road and turn right up the hill to Llanddona.

At the top of the rise, stone steps take you over a low wall and a little higher up a gate leads onto a track beside a house

Look back at this point for a final view of Red Wharf Bay with the resorts of Benllech and Moelfre beyond and in the far distance the lighthouse at Point Lynas. The little hills of Mynydd Bodafon and Parys Mountain can also be seen.

Follow the track past the house and at a gravel road turn right. Pass a radio mast on your right and keep right at the next two junctions. Eventually, you will arrive at the main road through the village, turn left here and return to point 1 bearing right by the Owen Glyndwr public house.

There is little of note at Llanddona, although its secluded location and fine views of Snowdonia make it an attractive spot. It will also appeal to those who dislike Anglesey's flat interior; the walk up from Red Wharf Bay should have convinced you that this area is anything but flat.

During earlier centuries the village was known for its witches. Exactly who these were is unknown and each account gives a different explanation, although the descendants of shipwrecked Irish sailors are thought to have settled in this remote corner and, due to their unfamiliar appearance and language, were most likely feared by locals. This fear and suspicion could well have been encouraged in an attempt to conceal smuggling activities which were almost certainly carried on here. Anglesey is thought to have been an intermediate stage for contraband runners from the Isle of Man.

3. Moelfre

Distance: *4½ miles*

Start: Begin the walk at the beach car park Traeth Lligwy. *Grid ref. 497 871 (Landranger 114, Pathfinder 735).*

The Route

1. From the car park turn right along the coastal path which is well defined and gives a fine view of the wide sweep of Traeth Lligwy with Ynys Dulas beyond. As you approach Porth Forllwyd, bear right through a kissing gate to avoid private land, before the path rejoins the coast to run along a series of low limestone cliffs.

On the approach to the small shingle inlet of Porth Helaeth, look to your right where a small stone memorial commemorates the wreck in 1859 of the Royal Charter. *"This stone commemorates the loss of the steam clipper* Royal Charter *which was wrecked on the rocks nearby during the hurricane of 26th October 1859 when over 400 persons perished. Erected by public subscription in 1935."*

The memorial overlooks the bay where the ship sank and can be approached by a short field path on the right, just before the beach.

In its day, the Royal Charter *was one of the fastest clippers on the run between Liverpool and Australia and her captain, Thomas Taylor, was justly proud of her. On August 26th 1859, she left Melbourne laden with a valuable cargo of gold and passengers who had made their fortune in the Australian gold fields. Eight weeks later she was almost within sight of Liverpool after a journey of over 16,000 miles when one of the worst storms of the century (which claimed a total of 133 ships and almost 800 lives) drove her onto rocks little more than a stones throw from here. There were survivors but very few; 465 lives were lost. The whole country was shocked by the disaster, particularly by the fact that no women or children were among the survivors and by rumours that locals had plundered bodies washed ashore in the days that followed.*

The dead were buried locally in the cemeteries of several nearby villages and Rev. Stephen Hughes, of Llanallgo reputedly wrote over 1,000 letters to the families and friends of those who perished.

One survivor, by the name of James Dean, was not only lucky enough to be washed ashore alive but also managed to keep hold of his fortune which he held in the form of a banker's draft wrapped in oilskin. He is said to have returned to Moelfre on the anniversary of the disaster for the remaining 36 years of his life to give thanks for his survival. His descendants carried on the practice for more than a century after the sinking.

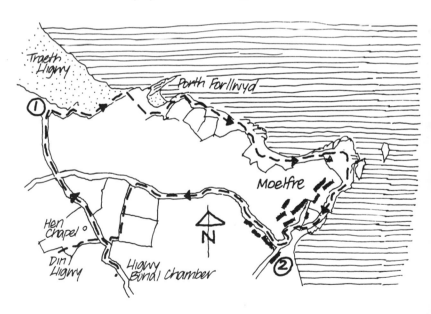

Beyond the cove, the footpath rises to a caravan site then bears left to continue along the coast to open land on the headland near the old coastguard lookout. Ignore signed footpaths to the right here, keeping instead to the edge of the rocks.

The lookout is well placed, commanding fine views to the north and east along the North Wales coast to the Great Orme with the mountains of Snowdonia on the skyline.

Continue around the headland with Ynys Moelfre to your right across the narrow channel of Y Swnt. Farther along, a kissing gate leads to a small shingle beach and at the far end you are directed right by a white cottage. Follow the path past the lifeboat station and Seawatch Centre which houses an exhibition of sea rescue, along with the RNLI lifeboat *Bird's Eye*.

This craft was presented to the RNLI by Birds Eye Foods Ltd and used for over 20 years between 1970 and 1990 in New Quay, Dyfed. It was launched 89 times and saved 42 lives.

Beyond the Seawatch Centre, the path bears right to Moelfre harbour. Join the road here and turn left along the front, then up the hill passing the Kinmel Arms on the right and the anchor taken from the wreck of the *Hindlea*, lost on October 27 1959 almost 100 years to the day after the loss of the *Royal Charter* and in almost the same location.

2. Take the first road on the right and continue for approximately ¾ mile.

Look for a quarry on your right once you have left the houses and cottages of Moelfre behind. Opposite the quarry entrance, stone steps on the left indicate the start of an unmarked field path. The right of way runs along the field edge, passing a second smaller quarry on your right. In the far corner of the second field, turn right and follow the field edge to a quiet lane.

Turn left here and follow the lane for about 300 yards to visit the Lligwy Burial Chamber which lies in fields to your right.

The most obvious feature of this burial chamber is the massive capstone: over eighteen feet long and nearly sixteen feet wide. It is estimated to weigh some 25 tons and was probably lifted into place with the aid of timber scaffolding. Two thirds of the chamber lie below ground level and make use of a natural fissure in the rock giving the chamber a very squat appearance. The entrance faces east towards the lane and originally the whole structure would have been covered by a mound of earth and stones which has been eroded away.

The Lligwy Burial Chamber

Excavations in 1909 revealed the unburnt remains of up to 30 individuals, as well as animal bones and pottery. The form and decoration of the pottery suggest that the chamber was in use during the late Neolithic and early Bronze Age periods.

Retrace your steps along the road passing the spot where you entered the lane. Beyond this, look for the signed footpath to Din Lligwy and Hen Chapel on the left. The path keeps beside the fence on your left with the ruins of Hen Chapel to your right. A metal kissing gate takes you into a small wood where a short rise leads to Din Lligwy.

Din Lligwy is one of the most remarkable and best preserved British settlements in the country and is thought to date from the middle of the fourth century, a period when the Romans were withdrawing from North Wales.

It is thought to have been the dwelling of a local chieftain or ruler and consists of a total of nine buildings; seven rectangular and two circular, which would originally have been thatched. The entrance is at the eastern end and a defensive wall some five feet thick surrounds the site which covers about half an acre. The two circular buildings are thought to have been dwellings, while the rectangular huts were most likely barns or workshops.

Retrace your steps to the lane passing Hen Chapel standing alone and isolated in the fields overlooking the bay.

Hen Chapel or 'Old Chapel' dates from the twelfth century when most early Celtic churches were built in stone for the first time. By this period, Anglesey was finally free from the fear of Viking raids and the lower parts of the walls survive from this time. The upper half of the walls were built 200 years later and additions were also made in the sixteenth century. Inside, the walls were originally rendered although little remains today. A short flight of steps leads to a small vault beneath the floor.

Turn left along the lane and at the crossroads go straight ahead returning to point 1.

4. Traeth Ora

Distance: *3½ or 6 miles*

Start: Begin at the beach car park, Traeth Lligwy. This lies at the end of a narrow lane running northwest from the A5025 at Brynrefail, between Moelfre and Amlwch.
Grid ref. 492 873. (Landranger 114, Pathfinder 735).

The Route

1. From the car park follow the coastal path to the left which runs north along the edge of the sand dunes at first, then traverses low rocks to a second bay, Porth-y-Mor (shingle).

Immediately ahead you can see the rocks of Ynys Dulas, which lie a mile or so offshore. The tower which can be seen, was built in 1824 as a beacon to identify the treacherous reef, of which the island is only a small part. The tower also incorporates a refuge for shipwrecked sailors and was kept stocked with food and provisions.

Traeth Lligwy from the south

Continue on the obvious path to Traeth Ora, a beautifully secluded sandy cove which cannot be approached by road. From here a footpath cuts through the bracken to the far end of the beach then bears left to Traeth Dulas, a small almost

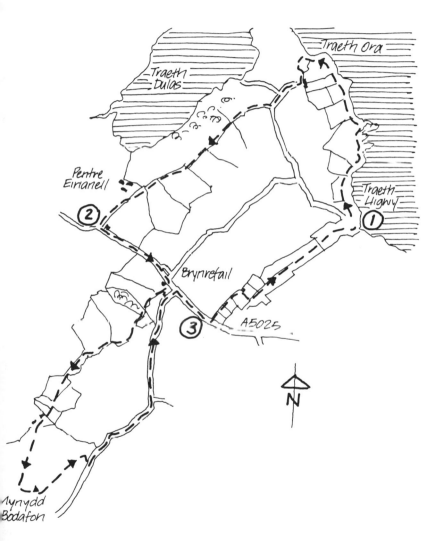

land-locked estuary. It is a beautiful spot and is well worth a visit but you must return to this point to continue the walk.

A well worn footpath on the left (right if you are returning from Traeth Dulas) rises to Penrhyn Farm. Bear right at the farm onto a track which eventually joins a tarmac road. Continue straight ahead up the hill and at the first bend bear right around the garden of a cottage, then left through a kissing gate into fields.

The right of way now rises directly through sheep grazed fields with the sands of Traeth Dulas just out of sight to the right. Higher up, the right of way stays close to the wall on your left until you enter a farm track by a gate or ladder stile. After about 300 yards, the track bears to the right and a stile directly ahead takes you into fields once more.

Keep right and after about 100 yards look for a ladder stile on the right near Pentre Eirianell. Beyond the stile, bear left along the field edge and continue to the Pilot Boat Inn.

2. Turn left and follow the road up the hill to Brynrefail.

Part way up the hill you will see a monument to the Morris brothers on your left. These four brothers grew up at Pentre Eirianell just below the Pilot Boat Inn in the early eighteenth century. They became famous for the many thousands of letters which they wrote to each other during their working lives, which have remarkably survived and give a fascinating glimpse of life in rural Wales, particularly Anglesey, during that period. Lewis Morris, the eldest of the brothers, is also noted for his sea charts which were published in 1784.

Where the road levels off there is a craft shop on the right. For a shorter round continue from point 3.

For a longer walk incorporating the excellent viewpoint of Mynydd Bodafon, turn right up a small ramp by the craft shop and church and walk about 100 yards along the old lane to where a stone stile leads into fields on the right. Bear

Looking towards Snowdonia from Mynydd Bodafon

left along field edges now following the right of way through a small wood. Beyond the trees, cut through an open field in the direction of a white cottage some distance away. After about 200 yards bear right beside the fence and head for a stile in the field corner.

In the next field keep to the field edge and rise to a second stile which leads into bracken covered grazing fields. Rise between the remains of a wire fence, then head for two stiles and a footbridge, keeping the summit of Mynydd Bodafon directly ahead. Cut directly through the following field aiming for a group of cottages and a stile in the far corner. Pass through a smaller field and finally a cottage garden ("Caer Mynydd"), where a gate leads onto a rough access track. Continue straight ahead here and at a T junction take the broad footpath directly ahead which cuts through the heather and gorse. Where the path levels out, bear left to the little rocky summit of Yr Arwydd.

Although it rises to a modest 584 feet, this little hill gives a fine panorama over Anglesey's predominantly flat landscape. Out to the west you can see Holyhead Mountain and Mynydd y Garn along with the collection of windfarms near Cemaes Bay. Nearer at hand you have the spoil heaps of Parys Mountain, where copper has been mined since prehistoric times and which fed a flourishing industry centred on Amlwch until the early nineteenth century.

At the eastern end of the island you will be able to see Puffin Island near Penmon Head along with the wide mouth of Red Wharf Bay, one of the largest bays in Anglesey.

To the south, the interior of the island is rather featureless although the basic structure - a series of shallow valleys running northeast to southwest, can plainly be seen. It is one of these valleys which, now flooded, forms the Menai Strait separating Anglesey from the mainland. A second valley running between Malltraeth and Red Wharf Bay almost divides the island in two, although much of it has now been reclaimed.

Back towards the mainland, the peaks of Snowdonia fill the southern skyline; from the rounded whale back slopes of the Carneddau in the east, to the sculptured pinnacles of Tryfan and Crib Goch on Snowdon. Farther west, the isolated hills of the Lleyn Peninsula stand plainly on the farthest skyline.

From the summit, head northeast over a second smaller hilltop and drop to a narrow access road. Turn right here then left at the lane and continue to Brynrefail. Turn right at the A5025.

3. After about 500 yards look for a signed footpath on the left which leads into fields. Keep to field edges following a line of stiles, then bear right though a gate by a large house. The path runs beside the garden to join a track by a gate. Turn left here, a stile and sign immediately ahead lead onto a well worn footpath. Follow this for some distance through gorse bushes to join a track. Bear left and follow the track back to point 1.

5. Llaneilian

Distance: *4½ miles*

Start: There is a small free car park at the end of the lane to Porth Eilian. *Grid ref. 477 929 (Landranger 114, Pathfinder 733).*

The Route

1. Turn right out of the car park and follow the lane down to the little sheltered cove of Porth Eilian. Here a narrow lane bears right and eventually leads to the lighthouse at the end of the headland at Point Lynas (Trwyn Eilian). Just before the long straight road to the lighthouse, the signed coastal path bears right over a stile. If you decide to walk out to the lighthouse, return to this point to continue the walk.

This long, finger-like headland has posed a threat to Liverpool bound shipping for over two centuries. The first beacon was built here in the early eighteenth century but the present lighthouse dates from 1835.

Cut through a rough grazing area with fields on the right until a kissing gate overlooking the water leads into a large field on the right. Bear half-left through the field to a ladder stile over the wall (ignore a lower stile over the fence). Continue straight ahead in the following field to a second kissing gate, bear right and rise with the hedge on your right to a third kissing gate in the top right-hand corner of the field. Cut diagonally left through the following field to the opposite corner where a ladder stile and a gate lead into a rough gorse covered grazing field.

Wooden steps lead up the bank and the right of way leads through gorse bushes to cross a farm track. Ignore this, instead continue to rise until you reach the fence which marks the upper edge of the field. Turn right here (arrow on post) and keep beside the fence to pass ruined farm buildings.

The white building to the left with a bay window facing the sea was previously one of the signalling stations which formed a communication chain between Holyhead and Liverpool. Messages of approaching shipping were relayed by means of visual numerical codes supported on movable arms.

A stile beside the buildings leads onto a prominent track and directly opposite stone steps lead up the bank. Climb the steps and follow the path beside a high stone wall on the left. At the end of the wall, turn right through a small field to a gate, then between old stone walls to join a metalled access road beyond a kissing gate. Rise to a quiet lane.

2. Turn right along the lane and continue to a T junction. Turn left here and after about 100 yards a signed footpath on the left leads through gorse and bracken to the triangulation pillar on Mynydd Eilian.

From this high point you have a grand view of the northeastern corner of Anglesey. South and east, the view takes in the Dulas Estuary and Moelfre with Red Wharf Bay and Penmon lighthouse in the distance. Over on the mainland, the mountains of Snowdonia, along with the Great Orme and the Clwydian Hills are also visible. In exceptionally clear conditions, you to be able to see the Isle of Man, the fells of the Lake District, the Lancashire coast and the mountains of southern Ireland.

Turning west, much of Anglesey's rugged northern coast is visible - from the lighthouse at Point Lynas past the harbour at Amlwch and the nuclear power station at Wylfa to The Skerries on the extreme northwestern tip of the island. Farther south, Holyhead Mountain can be seen along with the chimney of the aluminium works. In the far distance, the hills of the Lleyn Peninsula can just be seen over Anglesey's flat interior. Nearer at hand are the disfigured slopes of Parys Mountain, where copper has been mined since prehistoric times.

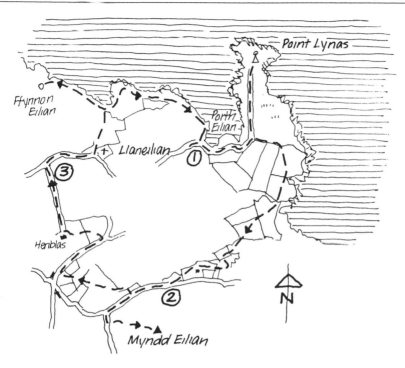

Retrace your steps to the road, turn right and at the first junction turn right again. After about 200 yards, look for a signed footpath on your left. Follow the path through a small field and over a stile. Turn left now and keep beside the wall at first, then cut through a large field aiming just to the right of the power station on the skyline. Cross a stile in the far corner of the field and follow the path through gorse bushes and a smaller field to a quiet lane at Pengorffwysfa.

Turn right down the hill until the lane bears left and a gate and ladder stile lead into fields on the left. Turn sharp left now through the field and make your way towards "Henblas", a large farmhouse immediately ahead. Just before the house turn right around the garden and join the drive by a cattle grid. Walk down the drive away from the house to the road and turn right.

3. Follow the lane to Llaneilian church (signed "Plas Eilian Camping and Caravan Site") and bear left towards the gate leading into the cemetery. Just before the gate, steps lead over the wall on the left. Shortly, two gates lead between buildings onto a concrete farm track with outbuildings to the right. Turn right here and where the track bends right, bear left down the bank to join the coastal path.

For a short detour to Ffynnon Eilian, turn left and continue to the next inlet. As you drop down to the stream, look to your left where a large rock lies beside the stream and to the left of this, a second large rock has a spring bubbling from beneath it.

Ffynnon Eilian is the well of Saint Eilian and remnants of a drystone wall enclosure can still be seen at the foot of the large rock from which the water flows. The well is said to run water long into a dry spell even when the nearby stream has dried up.

The well is also reputed to have been used as a cursing well by the locals. The recipient's name was written on a small tablet of stone and dropped into the water. The curse was thought to remain as long as the stone remained in the well .

Return along the coastal path to Porth Eilian. At the road turn right up the hill to point 1.

Llaneilian derives its name from Saint Eilian who is said to have landed at nearby Porth Ychain with his cattle and possessions in the sixth century and established the first church here. According to local legend, he obtained the land for his church from Caswallon Law Hir (Caswallon The Long Handed), a nearby lord whom he struck with blindness for some misdemeanour. Caswallon was later forgiven, his sight restored and out of gratitude (or fear!) he promised Eilian a piece of land to establish his church. It was agreed that Eilian would have all the land crossed by a deer of his choice before being caught by Caswallon's dogs.

   The chase started at Dulas and led towards Parys Mountain and Llan Carw (later known as "Harts Leap"), here the hart escaped by plunging into the sea. Thus Eilian acquired enough land to build his church and establish the settlement of Llaneilian.

Porth Eilian

6. Bull Bay

Distance: *4¼ miles*

Start: Take the A5025 west from Amlwch and two miles after leaving Bull Bay take the narrow lane on the right. After about ½ mile and just beyond a bend, park on the verge near two signed footpaths bearing the Coastal Heritage logo. This walk can be combined with route 7 Cemaes Bay to give a longer round.
Grid ref. 398 943 (Landranger 114, Pathfinder 733).

The Route

1. Take the first of the two signed footpaths (when approaching from the direction of the A5025). The right of way cuts directly through fields following a line of old iron kissing gates with the wide bay of Porth Wen to your left.

Lower down, the path enters an area of rougher grazing with gorse thickets and marker posts which enable you to keep to the path. Beyond a small footbridge, an old concrete ladder stile leads into fields again. Keep left around the field edge and look for a kissing gate on the left. Cut diagonally through the following field to a farmhouse known as "Castell". Keep to the right of the house and, ignoring a signed footpath to the right, keep straight ahead through a large gate which leads onto a short grassy track.

2. Where the track opens out into fields, bear left as indicated by the coastal footpath sign. The coastal path is narrow here but well worn and keeps close to the edge of the sea cliffs.

Porth Wen is a wide, unfriendly bay lined with steep cliffs and impressive rock scenery. With no real beach to absorb the impact of winter storms, the slaty rock has weathered into a series of jagged narrow inlets which cut in towards the footpath.

On the west side of the bay, you will see the abandoned remains of Porth Wen Brickworks with its tall chimneys and distinctive beehive shaped kilns. This enterprise used quartzite from nearby Craig Wen to make silica bricks for use in the steel industry. These were exported by boat from the little quay which can be seen adjacent to the works.

The existence of quartzite here possibly gave the bay its name; Porth Wen means 'white port' and Craig Wen, from which the white crystal was taken, means 'white crag' or 'white rock'.

As you approach Bull Bay, either turn right through an iron kissing gate and walk down the track to the Bull Bay Hotel, or continue straight ahead around the small headland which encloses the bay, to join a track beyond a house. After a few yards, turn left through a kissing gate and follow a narrow footpath with gardens to the right (bay to the left) to the Bull Bay Hotel on the right.

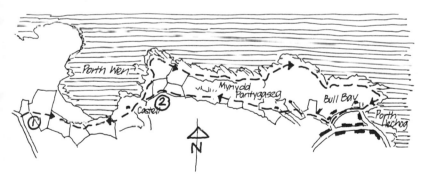

Out to the east of Bull Bay you will be able to see the little rock of East Mouse or Ynys Amlwch. It was on this rock that the huge steamship Dakota, one of the largest steamships to be wrecked on the Anglesey coast, ran aground and became a total wreck in 1877. Dakota *was almost 400 feet long and built for speed to cover the*

Looking across Porth Wen to the abandoned brick works

transatlantic crossing - a feature which led to her downfall. The ship was outward bound for New York and just a few hours into the journey when the order was given to turn away from the coast. For reasons which have never been fully explained, the ship turned the wrong way and headed straight for this treacherous northern coast. By the time the error was realised it was too late; the ship hit Middle Mouse rock and became a total wreck. All 218 passengers were rescued by the Bull Bay Lifeboat but the reasons for the helmsman's error remain a mystery.

Continue straight ahead (or turn right if you came down the track) up the lane and at the top of the rise turn right down the "Private Road to Bryn Arthur and St Eleth". Just before "Bryn Arthur" bear left onto a signed footpath which leads into fields. Bear half-left through the field to a stile beside a metal gate which leads onto a track. Turn right along the track and look for an iron kissing gate in the wall on the left just before a large house ("Ty Gwyn"). Cut directly through two small fields to join a second access road with a house to the right. The right of way continues opposite, where a gate leads into fields once more. Keep right around the field edge and in the top corner of the field go through a gap in the wall.

Directly ahead now you will see a small stone pillar and a gap in the ruined wall. Go through the gap and follow the right of way along the crest of a rounded rocky ridge (Mynydd Pantygaseg) for several hundred yards.

As you start to descend, with the wide bay of Borth Wen ahead, look for a kissing gate in the lower left corner of the field. Go through the gap and keep left beside the wall for some distance, following it as it bends leftwards to join a short track by a three fingered sign close to the cliff edge. Retrace your steps now past the farm ("Castell") and through the following grazing fields back to point 1.

7. Cemaes Bay

Distance: 6¼ *miles*

Start: There is a small car park with WC facilities near the harbour in the village of Cemaes Bay.
Grid ref. 373 935 (Landranger 114, Pathfinder 733).

The Route

1. From the car park, proceed eastwards along the seawall to a second car park at the end of a narrow lane. From here, turn left onto the signed "Cliff Path" which quickly climbs onto the low cliffs overlooking the bay.

Looking back you will see both the old and the new. For almost two centuries man has tried to harness one of Anglesey's most abundant energy resources - the wind. The little white towers of early windmills on the outskirts of the town are now dwarfed by the giant blades of the modern windfarms which turn slowly on the exposed hillside behind the village.

A good footpath weaves along field edges to Porth Padrig, Cemaes most easterly sandy beach and too far from local facilities to be overcrowded. Here you can make a short detour onto the sand or bear right to where a kissing gate leads into a quiet lane. Turn left now and follow the lane to the tiny church of Saint Badrig.

The church is dedicated to Saint Patrick, who was sent to convert the Irish by Pope Celestine in the fifth century and reputedly stands on one of the oldest Christian sites in Wales, possibly dating from as early as AD 440. How Saint Patrick came to build a church here is not clear but local legend maintains that he founded it in gratitude for his safe arrival ashore, after suffering a shipwreck on nearby Ynys Badrig. Porth Badrig is the supposed location of his landing after which he found shelter in a cave, now known as Ogof Badrig.

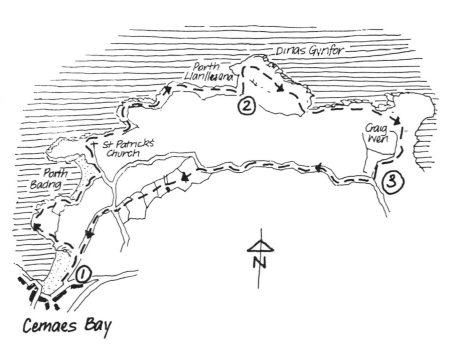

Cemaes Bay

The present building is a small structure, just 60 feet by 14 feet and stands on the very edge of the cliffs, defying the frequent winter gales which sweep in from the Irish Sea. It is mainly of sixteenth century construction although sections of the interior may date from medieval times.

In 1884 it was restored by Lord Stanley of Alderley, whose work showed the influence of his recent conversion to the Muslim faith. Much of his work was destroyed by fire in 1985, although recent renovation has allowed it to be open to the public once more.

Beyond the church, the cliffs turn eastwards and the walk becomes considerably more rugged. A gate beside the church leads back onto the cliff path which skirts the walled cemetery overlooking the sea. A stile beside the wall leads onto the cliff path proper, follow this until you are forced to bear left to a wire fence above an overhanging rock.

51

The tiny church of Saint Patrick

The path is poorly defined now but bears left along the outside edge of a ruined wall. After dropping steeply you head eastwards again before rising once more. Just before the top of the next rise, a narrow footpath establishes itself on the left and from now on the way is quite clear.

Although the path is much more obvious now, you will still need a sure foot and steady head to traverse these slopes, which can be treacherous in poor conditions. This is no place to allow adventurous children to wander! Don't be tempted to seek what appears to be easier ground higher up the slope, this will only lead you into greater difficulties.

As you round the headland, the little bay of Porth Llanlleiana comes into view and the angle soon eases. Ahead, a final knoll forces you to the right through bracken to a stone wall which soon leads you to the ruins of Porth Llanlleiana.

These ruins are one of the many relics from Anglesey's industrial past which dot this now deserted coastline. In addition to the crumbling buildings there are traces of a small port used to export locally dug china clay.

2. Behind the ruins, a footpath strikes out diagonally to the left up the steep hillside. Although quite steep, the toil is soon over and you are left with an easy stroll through heather and bracken to another ruinous building; the old lookout on Dinas Gynfor, Wales' most northerly headland.

The lookout is well sited, from here you can see almost the entire northern coast, from Point Lynas in the east to The Skerries off Carmel Head. Between lies some of the wildest and most unspoilt coastline on the island.

The defensive possibilities of Dinas Gynfor were exploited in prehistoric times when the summit was enclosed to form a fortress some 700 metres by 300 metres. The site was well chosen, even today the high plateau is only approachable with ease at its eastern end where the coastal path drops to Porth Cynfor.

From the lookout, an easy path leads through the heather before dropping steeply to Porth Cynfor (Hell's Mouth). Ahead, steps lead back to clifftop level and the angle eases once more.

Ahead you will see the old winding gear from Porth Wen Brickworks situated lower down on the hillside. Farther along, the crumbling chimneys and kilns overlook Porth Wen, a wide picturesque bay which marks the eastern limit of our walk. Today these enterprises seem strangely out of place in such otherwise unspoilt terrain, yet there are many such relics as we have already seen at Llanlleiana and we have our twentieth century counterpart in the form of nearby Wylfa Nuclear Power Station.

On a less grim note, the beacon mast to your left, situated on Torllwyn, is used by shipping, along with its counterpart on Porthllechog to the east, to determine an exact nautical mile.

Bear right beyond the winding gear and follow a grassy track above the ruins with a wide view of Porth Wen. Beyond a gate, a good footpath leads to a quiet lane.

3. Turn right along the lane and continue for almost 1 mile. Just beyond a bend, a sign and stile indicate a field path on the left. Cut through the centre of the fields (footbridge), aiming tc the right of a farmhouse where a stile leads onto an access track. Immediately ahead, a second stile leads into fields once more. Keep left to a kissing gate, then follow the well defined footpath beside a wire fence for some distance. At the lane turn right, then after a few yards turn left and return along the lane to Cemaes Bay and point 1.

8. Cemlyn Bay

Distance: *3¼ miles*

Start: There is a car park and information board at the eastern end of Cemlyn Bay. This is approached via a narrow lane which leaves the A5025 at Tregele opposite the Douglas Inn. *Grid ref. 336 932. (Landranger 114, Pathfinder 733).*

The Route

1. From the car park turn left along the beach (Esgair Cemlyn).

The unusual formation of the beach has been caused by centuries of onshore winds, depositing stones and shingle across the mouth of the bay to form a ridge (esgair). This has created a brackish lagoon on the landward side fed by fresh water and inundated by the sea only on the highest tides. Water level in the lagoon is maintained by a weir at the far end of the beach built in the 1930s and repaired in 1978.

The lagoon was managed as a private wildlife refuge for 40 years until the National Trust bought it with funds from Enterprise Neptune in 1971. The area is now leased by North Wales Wildlife Trust who maintain it as a nature reserve.

Unsurprisingly, the pool is a haven for wildlife and supports large numbers of Grey Mullet along with a variety of wildfowl including: Mallard, Shelduck, Redshank, Oystercatcher, Redbreasted Merganser, Coot, Little Grebe and Tufted Duck.

Of particular note is the Tern colony, which is one of the largest in Britain and returns here each spring to breed. The reserve provides a unique opportunity to view a Tern colony at such close quarters, although you are requested to follow the viewing instructions so as not to disturb birds during the breeding season. Please do not walk along the grass bank by the pool between April and July when the birds are nesting.

At the far end of the beach, cross a small stone footbridge which leads over the outlet stream from the lagoon (during high tides this may not be possible). Turn right now and walk over flat rocks beside a high wall and deserted farmhouse on the left. At the end of the wall bear left onto a gravel track and turn right. This leads onto the National Trust land at Trwyn Cemlyn.

Just before this, there is a stone memorial on the right to com-memorate the 150th anniversary of the first lifeboat on Anglesey (1828-1978). This was founded by the Reverend James Williams and his wife Frances after witnessing the wreck of the Irish Packet **Alert** *which drifted onto West Mouse killing 145 people in 1823. The Reverend and his wife are said to have watched helplessly from this headland as the packet ship foundered, leaving only seven sur-vivors.*

James and Frances devoted the rest of their lives to the forma-tion of the Anglesey Association for the Preservation of Life from Shipwreck. James was awarded the first RNLI Gold medal in Wales, after playing a major role in the rescue of sailors from the vessel **Active,** *wrecked in Cemaes Bay in 1835. Ironically, it was not at*

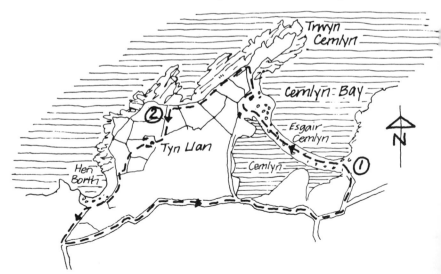

Cemlyn Bay from the coastal path

the helm of his lifeboat but from the shore, where he used his horse to get deeper into the surf and throw a grappling iron to the wreck, thus saving the lives of five men.

Here you can either walk over rough grass to the end of the headland for a view of the bay, or bear left following the wall to a corner overlooking flat wave cut rocks, where stone steps lead into fields on your left. The path now keeps tight against the right-hand field boundary, overlooking the sea to your right.

At low tide there is a panorama of wave cut platforms and small islands out towards The Skerries. On a blustery day, there is a strong Hebridean feel to this remote weather-beaten corner of Anglesey, which stands in sharp contrast to the softer south and east coasts.

These notorious reefs have been a hazard to shipping for centuries and caused the wreck in 1854 of the steamer Olinda *which hit Harry Furlough's Rocks and broke up. Fortunately, all those on board were rescued by the Cemlyn Lifeboat.*

Follow the coastal footpath through a line of kissing gates to a gateway with large round stone posts.

2. Turn left just before the gate and follow a grass track to join the access drive to "Tyn Llan". Turn right along the drive and pass through the farmyard to a gate beside the farmhouse. Go through the gate and cut through a small square field to the tiny church of Saint Rhwydrus. Stone steps to the right of the church lead into the cemetery.

This tiny church dedicated to Saint Rhwydrus sits isolated in the fields and its simple form and plain interior seem to have become part of the landscape. The font and nave date from the twelfth century and the chancel dates from a century later. In the little cemetery surrounding the church there are a number of graves from eighteenth and nineteenth centuries, with at least one dated 1676.

Return to the steps, turn left and go through a large gate at the end of the wall. Turn left around the field edge and rejoin the coastal footpath, turning left again over a stile. Drop to Hen Borth where a small shingle bank backs the bay. At the far end of the beach pass through two kissing gates and follow a faint path which leads away from the coast with a stream on the left. Farther on, pass through a second kissing gate and cross the stream by a small footbridge, which leads to the road. Turn left along the lane.

From the lane you can look left towards the little church and the bay at Hen Borth. The landscape on this part of the island is composed mainly of glacial drift and boulder clay, creating a series of hummocks or 'drumlins' covering the bedrock. This covering has been easily eroded by the sea, which can be seen to dramatic effect to the left of the church, where a drumlin has been cut almost in two at its highest point.

Keep straight ahead beyond "Fronddu" and at a T junction turn left. Turn left again at a fork after about 300 yards and walk along the lane back to the car park at point 1.

9. Carmel Head

Distance: *5 miles*

Start: There is a small National Trust car park (free) near the Mynachdy Estate. This is approached by following the lane to Cemlyn Bay (see route 8) but instead of turning right down the short lane which leads to the bay, take the next right. Where the lane bears right down to Trwyn Cemlyn after about ¼ mile, keep left. The car park is on the right after ¾ mile just before a sharp left-hand bend.
Grid ref. 317 926 (Landranger 114, Pathfinder 733).

The Route

1. Turn right out of the car park and go through the kissing gate immediately on the right, which leads onto the National Trust property at Mynachdy (information board). Follow the right of way over a small footbridge, through a second kissing gate and along the field edge to join the coastal footpath at the little bay of Hen Borth. Turn left here and follow the coastal path which well marked to Carmel Head - almost 2 miles.

This wild treacherous coastline lies on the busy shipping lane to Liverpool and has thus been a major hazard to shipping for centuries. This was particularly true during the age of sail, when numerous ships were driven onto its notorious reefs and islands by onshore winds. Ironically, one of the most famous wrecks was caused by a lack of wind when the Irish Packet Alert *drifted onto West Mouse after running out of wind while rounding Carmel Head. The Reverend James Williams of nearby Llanfairynghornwy and his wife Frances watched helplessly as 145 people drowned. They were so distraught by the tragedy and their inability to help that they established the first lifeboat in Wales at Cemlyn in 1828.*

Northwest of Carmel Head lies the group of rocks known as The Skerries - a Norse name derived from the word 'sker' meaning 'steep rock'. In Welsh they are known as Ynysoedd y Moelrhoniaid or 'Seal Islands' and were the scene in 1675 of the wreck of Britain's first Royal Yacht, the Mary *presented to Charles II. The remains of this ship were found by accident in 1971 in 40 feet of water.*

Originally, The Skerries were owned by Bangor Cathedral but were diverted into private ownership by Bishop Nicholas Robinson during the 1570s. In 1713, the islands were leased by a descendant of the Bishop's to William Tench. He built the first beacon here in 1716 and planned to collect duties from shipping entering Holyhead, however the venture proved to be disastrous and he died penniless in 1725. Tragically, he also lost his son who drowned while ferrying coal to The Skerries to keep the beacon running. Another tragedy happened to a descendant of Bishop Robinson on the 20 June 1739, when William Robinson and twelve companions drowned while returning from the beacon. Their empty boat was washed ashore four days later at Whitehaven in Cumbria.

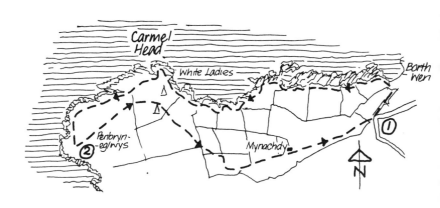

After a long and troubled history The Skerries became the last privately owned lighthouse in the country and was eventually sold for £444,984 11s 2d in 1841.

A rather curious wreck occurred at Carmel Head in the early 1740s, when an unknown vessel sank leaving two young boys as the only survivors. They came ashore lashed to a raft but as they could speak no Welsh or English, they could tell their rescuers nothing about the ship or its crew. One of the boys was adopted by a local family and given the name Evan Thomas. Evan eventually learned to speak Welsh and found that he had a gift for the setting of bones, which he later developed into a successful business. His descendants founded the Robert Jones and Agnes Hunt Orthopaedic Hospital near Oswestry. Nothing is recorded about the second youngster but both boys are assumed to have been Spanish.

Other links with shipping can be seen farther along the coast in the two large beacons known as the White Ladies. These line up with a similar tower on West Mouse, to act as a guide for shipping negotiating Carmel Head.

Continue west along the coastal path from Carmel Head, taking care around a number of deep inlets cut into this exposed headland. The path is faint here and there is more than one trail, although all seem to lead in the same direction. Continue until Holyhead Mountain comes into view and the coastal slope steepens considerably. Bear left here up the slope, then curve right to a prominent rocky top above Trwyn Cerrigyreryr.

From here there is a wide view of Holyhead Bay. To the southwest you will see the Irish ferries arriving and leaving Holyhead Harbour as they have done for centuries. Today however, this once hazardous and major undertaking can be completed quite safely in under two hours. Behind the town, Holyhead Mountain rises to over 800 feet, the highest point on the island. Further south the chimney at the aluminium works forms a prominent and well known landmark. On clear days, or just before sunset, you can often see the hills of southern Ireland on the western horizon.

Following the coastal path to Carmel Head

To the south, the coast becomes less dramatic beyond Church Bay, although the coves between Carmel Head and Porth y Bribys present some of the grandest sea cliff scenery on the island. The wide panorama from this hilltop was first exploited by the Romans, who are thought to have built a beacon and lookout on the summit of nearby Penbrynyreglwys, to guard the entrance to their harbour at what is now Holyhead.

2. Head back to the mine ruins seen earlier. These are not visible yet and there are few trails to follow, so cut across the open hillside aiming just to the right of the beacon on West Mouse until the ruins come into view. The chimney is the first to be seen along with a view east along the north coast.

The mines date from a boom in the copper industry during the eighteenth century, although there is evidence of mining here in prehistoric times.

Pass between the ruins on your right and the chimney on the left and pick up a grass track which contours the hillside to a gate beyond the White Ladies beacons. Beyond the gate, follow the track through a larger grazing field to a gate and stone steps in the far corner. The path forks here; bear right to a ladder stile about 150 yards away and turn left onto a track which curves to the right around a small artificial pool backed by conifer woods. Follow the track towards farm buildings at Mynachdy and pass through the farmyard to a gate immediately ahead. Go through the gate and follow the obvious track through grazing fields back to the lane at point 1.

Until quite recently, access to this part of the coast was very restricted having few public rights of way. In 1986 the National Trust bought 412 acres of the Mynachdy Estate with support from the Countryside Commission and have opened the area to the public, however, access to parts of the coast is only permitted between 1 February and 14 September.

10. Church Bay

Distance: *4½ miles*

Start: Free parking, a beach cafe and WC are all available at Church Bay, signposted off the A5025 at Llanfaethlu. *Grid ref. 301 892 (Landranger 114, Pathfinder 733).*

Note: Sections of this route within the Mynachdy Estate are closed to the public between 14 September and 1 February each year.

The Route

1. Turn left out of the car park and walk down the lane towards the beach. Just before the beach, bear right onto the signed footpath which backs the bay. Where the path runs into fields beyond a gate, keep to the left-hand field edge, then in the second field cut diagonally-right to the top corner (the coastal footpath keeps left here). There is a white cottage and a ruined building to the right here. Make your way through the gorse bushes directly ahead and higher up look for a stile and finger post in the wall and fence to your right. Cross the stile and turn left along a track passing a cottage on the left "Nant-y-Dwr".

Where the track bends sharp left, turn right for a few yards to where stone steps below a finger post lead over the wall on the left. Bear half-left to a rough wooden style on the external corner of a smaller field. Keep the fence to your right now and look for stone steps in the right-hand corner of the field. Walk directly through the centre of two larger fields now in the direction of a grey farmhouse. Bear left around the farm and join a track which cuts through the field to join a narrow lane with a bungalow and farm buildings to the left. Turn left and follow the lane for ¾ mile.

2. Where the lane bends sharp right, turn left onto a track which takes you into National Trust land at Mynachdy (identified by a small sign).

In 1986 the National Trust bought 412 acres of the Mynachdy Estate with support from the Countryside Commission. This enabled a large section of wild coastline to be opened to the public where previously there had been few public rights of way.

Much of this land is now managed as a pheasant rearing area, with a winter shoot providing the main income for the estate; because of this, access to footpaths within the estate is only permitted between 1 February and 14 September.

Follow the track beside conifer woods on the right down to the beautiful little cove at Ynys y Fydlyn.

This little cove with its shingle beach, crystal clear water and fine rock scenery is one of the most attractive locations on this part of the island. The remoteness of the cove probably means that you will have it to yourself, although you may be watched from the woods by thousands of young pheasants specially bred for the winter shoot.

At low tide it is easy enough to get onto Ynys y Fydlyn, from where you will be able to enjoy a fine view of the dramatic rock scenery which surrounds the cove. To the left, there is a huge sea cave and a marshy area which backs the bay (known as Llyn y Fydlyn). This was once a small inlet from the sea but has now become separated and has almost dried out. Both these features have been formed by the action of waves over the centuries, particularly during the winter months when strong westerly gales persist. Large sea caves like this can also be seen at North Stack on the exposed western coast of Holy Island.

Beyond Carmel Head, the lighthouse on The Skerries warns shipping of the treacherous rocks and reefs which reach out from Anglesey's northwestern tip. This coastline has been a hazard to shipping for centuries and has been responsible for literally hundreds of wrecks. One of the most notable was that of the Mary, *a 52 foot sloop which sank after hitting the rocks in thick fog in 1675. The* Mary *came from Amsterdam and was presented to Charles II, making it the first royal yacht. The* Hudiksvall, *a Swedish barque foundered on Ynys y Fydlyn in 1890 and the crew of 116 were forced to lash themselves to the upper rails until the Holyhead Lifeboat came to their aid. All lives were saved.*

3. Rise leftwards out of the bay to join the coastal footpath. The footpath is clear now although a little narrow in places and makes its way along the edge of the coastal slope. Beyond Porth y Bribys, the path cuts through fields using a permissive route marked by stiles, before joining the cliff edge once more. Take care not to miss the path as you round the last headland before Church Bay. This takes a line through the gorse and bracken, partway down the slope below fields on the left.

A kissing gate leads into fields above Church Bay and the outward journey can now be followed back to the car park.

Ynys y Fydlyn

11. Holyhead Mountain

Distance: *4½ miles*

Start: A free car park is situated opposite the "Hut Circle" sign just before South Stack.
Grid ref. 210 819 (Landranger 114, Pathfinder 734).

The Route

1. From the car park, follow the signs to Ellin's Tower, 500 yards or so across the heather.

This tower was built as a summer retreat for Ellin, the wife of William Stanley in 1867. Ellin was a keen observer of the bird life to be found around South Stack and her husband, who was the liberal MP for Anglesey from 1837-74, was responsible for several archaeological excavations on Holyhead Mountain. During their lifetime, the couple also provided Holyhead with a hospital, a home for sailors, the Market Hall and the town's water supply. Ellin died in 1876 and her husband joined her eight years later.

Ellin's Tower became a popular attraction in the closing years of the nineteenth and early twentieth centuries, before falling into decay after the World War II. In 1980 it was bought by the RSPB who carried out renovation work and opened it to the public as an information centre and bird hide in 1982.

Birds which can be seen here in large numbers include Guillemots, which favour the crowded, narrow ledges and Puffins, often found on the steep grassy slopes above the cliffs. Other birds commonly seen include Fulmars, Razorbills, Shags, Manx Shearwater and Herring Gull.

The cliff scenery directly below the tower and around the lighthouse at South Stack is amongst the most dramatic on Anglesey and a number of rock climbs have been recorded on the near verti-

cal cliffs below the tower. During the nesting months however, there is a climbing restriction to prevent disturbance.

From Ellin's Tower, take the steps up the hill to the road and turn left. The path to South Stack lighthouse passes through a white arch at the end of the road, but as the public are no longer permitted to cross the footbridge, this can only be used as a viewpoint.

If you decide not to view the lighthouse, bear right onto a well worn footpath which rises to a ruined building with commanding views of the surrounding coastline and a bird's eye view of South Stack and the lighthouse.

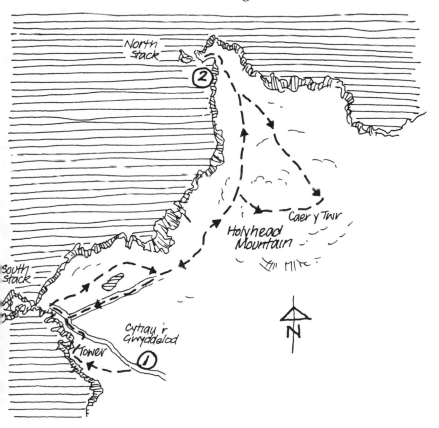

Rock climbing on the steep cliffs below Ellin's Tower

The ruins are the remains of the Holyhead Telegraph Station which stood at the western end of a chain of semaphore signalling stations linking Holyhead with Liverpool. It was installed by the Trustees of Liverpool Docks in 1827 and transmitted a message visually by means of movable arms. Although crude by modern standards, it was surprisingly effective when in use and in good conditions, could convey a simple message over a distance of 75 miles in just one minute.

Directly below you will see South Stack lighthouse, built in 1808 to provide a vital warning for the Liverpool shipping lane and the Irish Packet service. It was automated in 1984 and the public can no longer cross the footbridge onto the rock.

Behind the lookout, an obvious path continues along the rocky crest of a rounded ridge with a pond on the right and fine views northeast to North Stack and the massive cliffs of Gogarth.

Beyond this, bear right and rise to a narrow tarmac road. Cross over and follow a prominent gravel footpath with "dishes" to your left. At a high point on the path, there is a fork (rocky knoll immediately on left), the left path descends from here to the rock climbing area at Gogath, while the right fork leads towards the shoulder of Holyhead Mountain. As you approach the shoulder, stone steps lead up the rise. At the top, bear left and follow the path over a small minor summit with ruined drystone walling, before dropping steeply to North Stack. Join a prominent track just above the station and bear left.

Like South Stack, this rock has been separated from the mainland by the erosion of waves over thousands of years. If you walk down to the end of the rock opposite North Stack and look back, you will see a massive sea cave which will eventually create a stack out of the rock which you are now standing on. A number of high grade rock climbs have been recorded here and climbers can often be seen dotting the face to the right of the cave.

2. Retrace your steps up the hill (take care not to follow a lower path which is the coastal route to Holyhead) following a line of telegraph poles for a while. As the track begins to level, a narrow footpath curves to the right, follow this for some distance. Contour the hillside until you reach a level spot where the southwest coast of Holy Island around Trearddur comes into view, with the hills of the Lleyn Peninsula beyond. Turn right at a junction of paths and follow the meandering footpath to the summit of Holyhead Mountain.

As one would expect, this is a fine viewpoint with a spectacular panorama taking in almost the entire western side of Anglesey and Holy Island. To the north, you have the wide sweep of Holyhead Bay with The Skerries and Carmel Head in the far distance and the huge breakwater which shelters the harbour at Holyhead directly below. To the south and southeast, the view takes in the resorts and sandy bays of Trearddur, Rhoscolyn and Rhosneigr. On the horizon, the hills and rugged heights of Snowdonia stand above the flat green pastures of Anglesey's interior. Southwest, the hills of the Lleyn Peninsula can be picked out with Bardsey in the far distance. In clear conditions the Isle of Man and the hills of southern Ireland can often be seen.

This commanding view of the bay was evidently part of the attraction of the site to the Iron Age settlers who built the hillfort here, remains of which can still be seen. Throughout much of the Iron Age and the early post-Roman era, when this hillfort is thought to have been used, a major threat came from Irish tribes who sailed east to plunder the western coast of Britain.

The hillfort is known as Caer y Twr and extends over an area of 17 acres, making use of the hill's natural defences to the southeast and southwest. This is complemented by a wall around the northern perimeter some thirteen feet thick and still almost ten feet high in places. The entrance is at the northeast corner where the wall can be seen to turn inwards, forming an imposing passageway which could be easily defended.

Within the hillfort no hut circles have been identified, although the base of a Roman watchtower can be seen on the highest point next to the triangulation pillar. This was almost certainly linked to the Roman coastal fort at Caer Gybi (Holyhead) and is thought to have been used, along with a similar lookout on Penbrynyreglwys near Carmel Head, to guard the approaches to the fort and its harbour.

From the summit, take one of the paths which drop to the north to join the path used earlier. Turn left now and follow the gravel path back to the tarmac road. Turn left here and follow the road back to the lane which was used earlier to reach South Stack. Turn left and return to the car park at point 1.

Opposite the car park entrance a short path leads to a collection of prehistoric hut circles.

The site was originally excavated by William Stanley (who we have already mentioned in connection with Ellin's Tower) in the 1860s, when the remains of over 50 hut circles were recorded spread over an area of 15 to 20 acres. The settlement has come to be regarded as a classic Romano-British village, although later excavations and dating have revealed evidence of earlier habitation reaching back to the early Iron Age around 500 BC and perhaps even as far back as the Bronze or Stone Age.

The hut circles in evidence today, though not as numerous as those uncovered by the excavations of William Stanley, are remarkably well preserved and features such as entrances and internal stone furniture can be identified with ease. When in use, these stone circles formed the foundations on which wigwam-like huts with thatched roofs were erected.

12. Rhoscolyn

Distance: *2 or 4¼ miles*

Start: There is a free beach car park with WC facilities at Borthwen, Rhoscolyn.
Grid ref. 273 752 (Landranger 114, Pathfinder 750).

The Route

1. From the car park, make your way onto the beach and turn right along the sand, or, if the tide is high, follow the path along the top of a concrete wall which backs the beach. This leads back down onto the sand and about 200 yards farther on, a slipway rises on the right. At the top of the rise keep right at a fork and follow the track as it bends to the right. Look for a footpath sign which directs you along the drive to "Bryn Eithin". After about 20 yards, bear right into the garden of an adjacent house, then left onto a well worn path between and behind gardens.

Farther on, cross an access road where stone steps opposite lead over the wall into sheep grazed fields. Rise through the fields now, aiming for the coastguard lookout on the skyline.

From the lookout in clear weather there is a grand view over much of Caernarfon Bay. To the north, Holyhead Mountain with the lighthouse flashing at South Stack can be seen in the distance, along with the chimney of the aluminium works near Holyhead. Southwards lie the sandy coves and islets around Rhoscolyn, with Rhosneigr and the headland at Aberffraw across the channel on Anglesey.

On the mainland the peaks of Snowdonia line the horizon - from the Carneddau in the east to the Glyders, Snowdon and the

Nantle Ridge. Further west lie the hills of the Lleyn - Yr Eifl, Garn Fadryn, Mynydd Mawr, Mynydd Anlog and finally, Bardsey.

2. From the lookout, continue on the grassy path which cuts through sheep grazed fields to Ffynnon Gwenfaen (Saint Gwenfaen's Well). This lies near the edge of the cliffs about 600 yards away. Aim just to the right of the headland which runs west from Holyhead Mountain.

This is an ancient well which captures spring water below ground level. It has stone steps, corner seats and may originally have been roofed. During the Middle Ages it was a place of pilgrimage and was believed to have the power to cure mental illness.

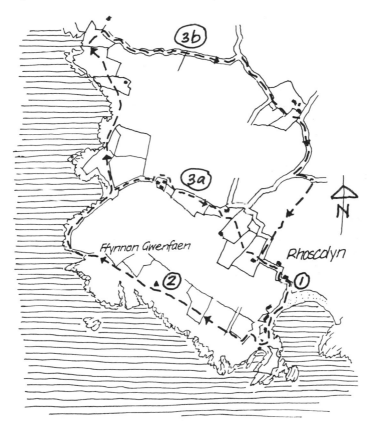

Beyond the well, pass through a kissing gate and follow the path along the top of a large crag overhanging the sea (take care here). The path stays close to the wall on the right and a rail protects the path at one point but the edge is never far away.

It was off this headland in 1855 that the Liverpool ship, Southern Cross *foundered and sank after striking a submerged rock in thick fog. The ship went down rapidly giving the crew of 17 just enough time to escape in the ship's lifeboat. Incredibly, this craft also struck rocks in the poor visibility and the exhausted men were*

Ffynnon Gwenfaen

forced to spend the next 12 hours on one of the many tiny rocks which can be seen breaking the surface. Their plight was noticed the following morning when the Rhoscolyn Lifeboat was sent to their aid.

Occasionally rescues ended in disaster, not just for those in trouble but also for the lifeboat crews themselves. This happened in 1920 when five Rhoscolyn volunteers including the Coxswain, Owen Owens, lost their lives in heavy seas after unsuccessfully going to the aid of the stricken steamer Timbo *in Caernarfon Bay.*

Follow the footpath into the next inlet where there is a little footbridge just beyond a stile.

At this point you have a choice. For a shorter round of about 2 miles continue from paragraph **3a**. Alternatively, the walk can be lengthened to 4¼ miles by continuing along the coastal path (paragraph **3b.**).

3a. Cross a stile to the right of the footbridge and cut through a small square field enclosure to pick up an old track enclosed by crumbling stone walls. Just before a large white farmhouse, turn left and follow the wall around the front of the house. In the field corner, bear half-right (arrow on post) to a kissing gate at the top of the field which leads onto the access drive. Turn left along the drive.

Just before Rhoscolyn church, turn right onto a signed footpath which follows the cemetery wall to a stone stile. Beyond this, cross a wide driveway with a large house to the right and climb over a ladder stile which leads into fields again. Bear half-right through the field to a kissing gate contained by stone walls. A similar gate in the far field boundary takes you across an access track and along the field edge to a small gate by a white cottage. A short enclosed footpath leads past a cottage to the lane used to reach the beach car park at the beginning of the walk. Turn right here and follow the lane back to the car park at point 1.

3b. Continue along the coastal footpath which shortly runs along the large crags which back the inlet (Porth Saint). Here the path veers half-right away from the cliff edge in the direction of the chimney of the aluminium works at Holyhead. Rejoin the coast and drop to a stile over the fence where a small inlet on the left contains a natural arch. Beyond this, make your way through an area of rocky outcrops to a small metal kissing gate. This is followed shortly by a second kissing gate which leads onto a gravel path. The path leads to a large wooden gate with stone pillars and a stile to the right. Cross the stile and bear left through a rough pasture field to a small metal kissing gate beside a small cove. Go through the gate and walk about 20 yards or so to the corner of the fence on your left and bear half-right towards a white house. Turn right along the access road to the house and continue for about ½ mile to a T junction.

Turn right here and follow the lane over a small bridge to a sharp right-hand bend by Rhoscolyn chapel, built in 1906. Go through a field gate immediately ahead (telephone box on left) and keep to the field edge with a small cemetery on the right. Bear left along the hedge in the top corner of the field and just before a small farmhouse, turn through a kissing gate to cut through a small field to the road.

Turn right along the lane and after some distance turn left into a narrow lane signposted "Silver Bay Holiday Park". After about 200 yards, a kissing gate on the right (beside the drive to "Coedan") leads into fields. Follow the well worn path through a small field, then between bracken covered banks to enter a larger field by a kissing gate. Cut through the centre of the field to another kissing gate and bear left along the field edge to pass a small white cottage. A short access track leads to the lane used earlier to reach the beach car park. Turn left now and follow the lane back to the car park at point 1.

13. Aberffraw

Distance: *5 miles*

Start: There is free parking available for a number of cars on common land beside the old bridge at Aberffraw. *Grid ref. 356 689 (Landranger 114, Pathfinder 768).*

The Route

1. Cross the old bridge and turn left immediately onto a track which runs beside the river. Where the track bears left onto the sand, continue along the shore to the mouth of the river.

If the water is high or the shore too wet, turn right onto a narrow footpath, then turn left between gardens. This path takes you back to the shore where a low wall runs above the sand. Follow the path along the top of the wall, then drop onto the sand just before a white cottage and continue to the river mouth.

Originally, Aberffraw was open to the sea and even enjoyed a brief period of prosperity as a small port. Over the centuries however, the estuary on which it lies has become filled with wind blown sand with the result that today over half a mile of sand dunes separate it from the sea. In its original state, the estuary would have been something like the nearby Malltraeth Sands and extended inland for over two miles. Llyn Coron, near Bodorgan Station, which is now a fresh water lake, marks the original limit of the estuary.

Today, you will find nothing at Aberffraw to suggest its past importance as the administrative centre for the kings and princes, not just of Anglesey, but the whole of North Wales. For eight hundred years, Welsh kings and princes used the royal palace at Aberffraw as a base in their fight against invasions from Irish, Saxons, Vikings and finally Normans.

The palace was established by Cunedda, who came down from Strathclyde with his sons and a large army of fighting men, to rid North Wales of barbaric Irish tribes who had attacked and overrun the kingdom, following the Roman withdrawal. Cunedda was a powerful Celtic chieftain who was able to pass on to his sons a vast kingdom which encompassed much of present day North Wales. His grandson, Cadwallon, who inherited the northern kingdom which would become Gwynedd, is credited with finally ridding Wales of Irish invaders in a last battle on Anglesey about AD 470. Other rulers associated with Aberffraw include Cadwallon's son, Maelgwyn Gwynedd, who granted land for the founding of monasteries at Holyhead and Penmon in the mid sixth century and Rhodri Mawr (Rhodri the Great 844-878), who ruled much of Wales

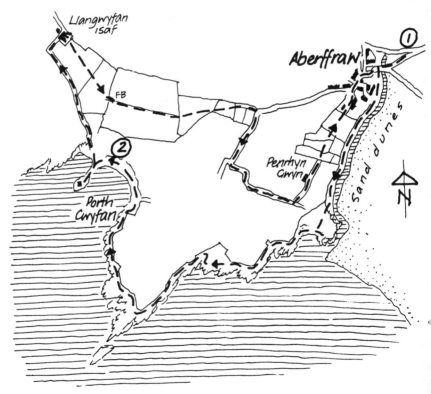

The village of Aberffraw

from his seat at Aberffraw, as did Llywelyn the Great. Other prominent names include Gruffydd ap Cynan who died in 1137 at the
remarkable age of 82, his son Owain Gwynedd and Llywelyn the
Last, whose defeat by Edward I in 1282 brought Welsh independence to an end.

With such a long period of use - something like the period which
separates our own time from that of Edward I, it is perhaps sur-
prising that no trace of the palace is now to be seen. The reason for
this is that throughout its long history it was built entirely from
wood, a fact which made possible its partial destruction by the
Vikings in 968. The building of castles and churches from stone
did not really begin until after the Norman conquest and even
then, the earliest motte and bailey castles were usually of timber
construction. Although this may seem strange as we look at the
bare treeless landscape of today, for much of the period that the
palace was in use, Anglesey was thickly wooded. By the fourteenth
century, timber was evidently in shorter supply, for we are told
that in 1317 the palace was demolished and its timbers used to
repair Caernarfon Castle.

81

Near the mouth of the river, bear right through a kissing gate onto the coastal footpath. Before you do this, walk left across the grass to the end of the little promontory for a fine view of the bay.

This is one of the most beautiful bays in Wales and is perhaps seen at its best on a clear summer evening when the crowds have left. Across the shallow clear waters of Caernarfon Bay, the blue outlines of Gryn Ddu, Yr Eifl and the hills of the Lleyn Peninsula line the horizon, while the higher peaks of Snowdonia peep over the headland at the end of the bay.

The coastal path from here is easy to follow and keeps to the edge of the low rocks with occasional departures into small coves and onto wave-cut rocks. Keep your eyes open for grey seals which can frequently be seen in these shallow waters. Continue to Porth Cwyfan, a wide bay with a tiny church on a small island. A short walk across the shingle beach takes you onto the island which is cut off at high tide.

This tiny isolated church dedicated to Saint Cwyfan, was founded in the seventh century and rebuilt in stone during the twelfth century. In the centuries that followed, it was added to a number of times before being fully restored in the nineteenth century. Despite this, it has managed to retain its original simple form. The stone wall which surrounds the island was built during the nineteenth century restoration to counteract severe erosion problems. Outside the church a few scattered gravestones remain from the eighteenth century, along with a memorial to Frank Morley, a youngster of 20 who drowned in nearby Porth Trecastle.

2. At the end of the beach, a track rises past a small bungalow to the old MOD camp at Ty-croes. Here the track bears right to a large derelict farm, "Llangwyfan-isaf". Turn sharp right through the farm, then cut through the centre of two fields to a kissing gate and stone footbridge. Follow the right of way along the field edge, cross over a farm track and make for a second footbridge straight ahead. Bear diagonally-left through a small walled field, then keep beside the wall to the lane.

Turn right, follow the lane to the first bend and bear left onto a track (footpath sign) which runs between fields for some distance. Follow the track past a derelict farmhouse, and at the next junction take the signed footpath on the left. After passing a farmhouse ("Penrhyn Gwyn") on your left, the path turns right down to the river and an iron kissing gate straight ahead marks the start of the field path back to Aberffraw which you should now take.

For those who would like to learn more about Aberffraw's history, a visit to Llys Llywelyn will be well rewarded. You can also learn about the work of the Anglesey Coastal Heritage Project which is centred there. The Project undertakes a great deal of work to both conserve the island's coastal heritage and to make it more accessible.

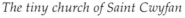

The tiny church of Saint Cwyfan

14. Ynys Llanddwyn

Distance: *8¼ miles*

Start: There is a small parking area in Newborough, about 200 yards along the lane which leads down to the beach at Llanddwyn, signposted "Traeth Llanddwyn". *Grid ref. 423 656. (Landranger 114, Pathfinder 768).*

The Route

1. Walk up the lane out of the village and look for a small church on the right. Walk down the short access track passing the church on its right-hand side and turn left onto a footpath which runs along the back of the cemetery. This path is frequently used and well worn.

Just before the conifers of the Newborough Forest, the path enters a large grazing field; cut directly through the field to a gate which leads into the trees. Follow the broad path through the plantation and where the path forks, keep right.

The Newborough Forest was planted in the 1950s to stabilise a vast area of moving sand dunes formed over the last 700 years by prevailing southwesterly winds. Today, it is a working forest producing over 10,000 tons of timber per year and has been designated as a Site of Special Scientific Interest.

The trees, mainly Corsican Pine, thrive in the sandy soil and are not harmed by the salt spray thrown up during winter storms. They have stabilised the dunes which have suffered frequent erosion problems over the centuries. As early as Elizabethan times, attempts to stabilise the dunes by planting marram grass were made after over-grazing damaged the thin soil cover. This led to vast areas of valuable agricultural land, which had been farmed since the Middle Ages, being buried by several metres of wind blown sand.

The introduction of marram grass gave rise to a thriving cottage industry making ropes, baskets and mats which lasted until the end of the last century. Today the lime rich soil (from tiny shell fragments) of the older inland dunes, produces a colourful display of wild flowers in the summer months.

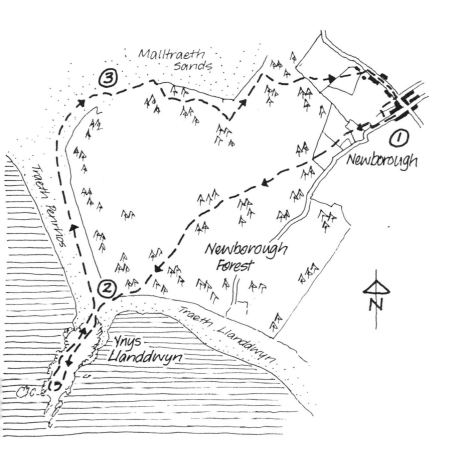

This sensitive area is now protected and managed by Anglesey Coastal Heritage and walkers are reminded to keep to the designated rights of way to avoid further erosion.

After about 1¼ miles there is an obvious bend to the right; keep straight ahead here and make your way to a small parking area almost on the edge of the forest. Either take the obvious track down to the beach and turn right along the sand to Ynys Llanddwyn, or bear right just beyond the parking area and follow a narrower footpath which passes a small clearing on the right to access the beach almost opposite Ynys Llanddwyn.

2. A short walk across the sand takes you onto the island. Aim for a large information board and follow the track immediately behind the board down to the Pilots' Cottages near the old lighthouse.

The goat-like sheep which can be seen grazing small enclosed fields just before the Pilot's Cottages, are Soay sheep said to be one of the oldest surviving breeds in the world. They are still found semi-wild on St Kilda off the northwest coast of Scotland and are believed to have been used by Neolithic and Bronze Age settlers in Britain and Northern Europe.

Overlooking the bay at the southern tip of the island are a number relics from the island's maritime past. The row of tiny cottages to the right of the path once housed the famous Llanddwyn Pilots and their families. These individuals took turns to man the lighthouse, built in 1845 and now abandoned, and guide shipping into nearby Caernarfon harbour. They also acted as lifeboat men and carried out a number of daring rescues during the nineteenth century. The small canon which stands in front of the cottages was used throughout this period to summon the lifeboat and crew in times of distress. The Pilots' Cottages were renovated in 1977 by Anglesey Borough Council and two are regularly open to the public where an exhibition and a series of period rooms can be viewed.

The smaller white tower down to the left was originally a navigation beacon built in 1819. In 1972, this structure was found to be more suitable for the modern automatic beacon than the lighthouse which is now disused.

Part of the exhibition tells the story of Saint Dwynwen, who is said to have lived here in the fifth century and gave the island its name. In her younger days, Dwynwen fell in love with a prince by the name of Maelon, who was so infatuated by the young maiden that he could not wait for marriage and tried to seduce her. The resistance she made resulted in Maelon's rejection.

Outside the Pilots' Cottages, Ynys Llanddwyn

The story says that while she mourned her loss, an angel visited her and gave her a healing potion, which cured her of her love and turned Maelon into ice. Dwynwen then vowed never to marry and to become a nun.

The shrine which she established here attracted pilgrims in great numbers in the years that followed, particularly from the love sick. She is said to have used the magical powers of a secret well to determine whether or not a loved one was faithful.

This story is a fine example of how the superstitions and beliefs of the old Celtic religion quickly found their way into the early Christian church. References to healing potions, magic wells and wicked princes being turned into ice, echo the stories of the Mabinogion, a series of folklore stories which predate Christianity by several centuries.

Today, spectacular scenery and miles of secluded beach are the main attraction for the visitor. To the south, the serrated outlines of Snowdonia, followed by the blue silhouettes of Yr Eifl (The Rivals) and the smaller hills of Lleyn form an impressive backdrop to the wide sweep of Caernarfon Bay and the golden sands of Traeth Llanddwyn.

From the old lighthouse, a good footpath leads along the northern edge of the island passing the ruins of Eglwyseg Dwynwen on the right.

These are the ruins of a sixteenth century church dedicated to Saint Dwynwen, said to be built on the site of her original church established over 1,000 years earlier. The arched windows are edged with sandstone blocks and the outline of a small churchyard can be traced in the grass outside the building. The present ruinous state of the church is said have been due in part to the removal of timbers for boat building and stone for the navigation beacon at the beginning of the nineteenth century.

Leave the island and turn left along Traeth Penrhos, one of the grandest and most isolated beaches in Anglesey. Follow the sand for about 1¼ miles, before the dunes become lower and curve northeast into the vast expanse of Malltraeth Sands, the tidal estuary of Afon Cefni.

Part way along the beach, the remains of a wreck can often be seen breaking the waves at low tide. This is known locally as Y llong Groeg, meaning "The Greek Ship". She was the brig Athena, which foundered in December 1852 en-route to Liverpool. 14 crew were saved from the wreck by the Llanddwyn lifeboat.

This vast stretch of tidal sands was the inspiration for much of the work of the late wildlife illustrator Charles Tunnicliffe. He was born in 1901 in eastern Cheshire and moved to Malltraeth with his wife in 1947. His house "Shorelands", looked out over the estuary and provided the naturalist with enough material to last him a dozen lifetimes. He died at Malltraeth in 1979.

Large as the estuary is today, originally it reached over 12 miles inland almost to the outskirts of Llangefni. Like Traeth Mawr near Porthmadog, reclamation schemes at the beginning of the nineteenth century turned much of the estuary into farmland. This was accomplished by means of a seawall or "cob", which spans the sands near Malltraeth.

The estuary is of national importance to the numerous species of wild fowl which stop to feed here on their long migratory flights between Arctic Norway and Africa.

3. Just before the final small dune, bear right onto a path through the dunes to join a sandy track which runs along the edge of the forest. Turn left along the track and continue, with the trees on your right and the salt marshes on your left, for about 1 mile.

A few hundred yards after entering the woods proper, turn left at an obvious T junction. Follow the broad forestry road until you can make a right turn opposite a wooden lookout tower on the left. Make a short rise now passing the ruins of a small building on the left and where the track levels off and bends to the right, take a grassy path directly ahead. This passes some dark, peaty pools on the right before leaving the woods to enter grazing fields.

Cut half-right through the field aiming for the houses in Newborough on the brow of the hill. Keep to the right of a marshy area in the centre of the field. A ladder stile crosses the fence by a stream which can be difficult to negotiate during a wet spell.

Make your way diagonally-left through the following field to a stone stile in the far corner below a group of small conifer trees. Keep left along the wall for a few yards, then turn left through an old iron gate and pass through the garden of a bungalow to enter a small cul-de-sac. At the A4080, turn right and walk along the road into Newborough.

This rather ordinary Welsh village came into existence in 1303, to accommodate the villagers evicted from Llanfaes when Edward I began the building of his new garrison town at Beaumaris. The move created a "new borough" from which the village gets its name. However, the exposed location soon created problems for the villagers. Over-grazing and the removal of trees on the nearby dunes of Newborough Warren soon damaged the delicate soil cover and by the time of Elizabeth I, wind blown sand had buried much of the village's valuable agricultural land.

In an attempt to stabilise the dunes, marram grass was introduced which, in the nineteenth century, gave rise to a flourishing basket and rope making industry.

Opposite the turning to "Llangaffo B4421", which is the first road on the left as you enter the village, turn right down a short access road. Just before a bungalow ("Pengwern"), bear right (straight ahead) onto an enclosed footpath. Follow the footpath until a kissing gate leads onto a farm track. Turn left here and at the lane turn left again returning to point 1.

15. Brynsiencyn

Distance: 5 *miles*

Start: Begin the walk in the village of Brynsiencyn, situated on the A4080 about 5½ miles from Menai Bridge. There is a small free car park and WC opposite Y Groeslon Hotel. *Grid ref. 484 671 (Landranger 114, Pathfinder 768).*

The Route

1. Turn right out of the car park and walk down the narrow lane to Llanidan (about ½ mile).

Opposite the entrance to Llan Idan Farm, turn right over a stone stile into a large field. Bear half-right through the centre of the field to where stone steps and a tiny iron gate lead over the wall in the corner of the field. Make your way through a small overgrown quarry, keeping to the right of undergrowth for ease. Beyond the quarry look for stone steps over the wall, which lead into fields once again.

The right of way keeps to the left-hand field edge in the first two fields, then directly through the centre of the remaining fields. Stone steps beside pine trees lead over the wall and onto the shore of the Menai Strait.

2. Turn right now and walk along the beach to the lane. Follow the road which runs parallel to the shore to the Mermaid Inn, near the old pier from which the Tal-y-foel Ferry ran to Caernarfon.

Tal-y-foel was one of many small ferries which carried passengers across the Menai Strait for centuries before the bridges were built. In the days before Thomas Telford built the A5 and the graceful suspension bridge which carries it onto Anglesey, this quiet corner of the island would have been busy with passengers travelling to and from Caernarfon. Another ferry ran from Cáernarfon to Abermenai Point, a sand-bar at the mouth of the strait near Newborough.

Though a journey of less than two miles, the crossing was always dangerous and there have been at least two major tragedies here. The first was in 1664 when, with 80 passengers on board, the ferry capsized following a dispute over fares. There was only one

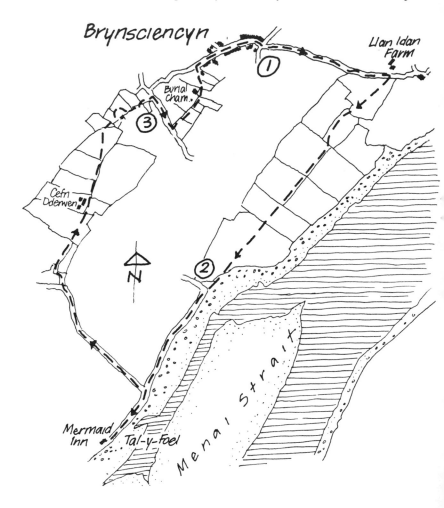

survivor to tell the tale. When they heard of the tragedy, the people of nearby Newborough were convinced that the sinking was divine punishment. It seems that timbers removed from the disused church at Llanddwyn had been used in the building of the ferry.

Over 120 years later in 1785, a particularly sad incident occurred to the same ferry bound for Abermenai Point. Here the strait is at its widest and being relatively shallow has several sand banks which dry out at low tide. The narrow channels between the banks are the only safe route for boats making the crossing near low water. On 5 December, the ferry left Caernarfon with 55 passengers on board about one hour before low water. About half way across the boat ran aground and with a strong wind coming up the strait all attempts to re-launch her failed. She filled with water on the incoming tide leaving all the passengers stranded on sand banks shortly to be submerged. Their cries for help were eventually heard from the shore and a number of boats went to investigate. Unfortunately, all were too large to get close enough to save them in the shallow water. The would-be rescuers were powerless to help as one by one they were swept away by the icy waters. There was just one survivor - a man named Hugh Williams from Aberffraw who was washed ashore over two hours later.

Beyond the Mermaid Inn there is no public right of way although walkers can make their way along the shore with care and this route is used by the coastal path. Turn around now and return along the lane, taking the first road on the left. Follow this for about ½ mile.

Where the lane bends to the left just beyond a large white house, turn right through a large gate. Turn left immediately and pass through a second large gate into a small narrow field. Keep to the left and join a short track enclosed by hedges and the remains of a wall. At the end of the track, an old iron gate leads into fields. Keep to the right-hand hedge and beyond a gate, cut through the centre of a field to the abandoned "Cefn Dderwen Farm".

An aerial view of Caernarfon and the Menai Strait

There are two gates in front of the farm; take the right-hand gate and pass through the yard with the house on your left. Beyond the buildings, a short overgrown track enclosed by crumbling walls leads into a large field. Keep to the right-hand field edge and where the wall bends right slightly, bear half-left through the centre of the field to an old iron kissing gate. Pass through the gate, keeping right to a second gate which leads onto an enclosed footpath with a farm to your right. Cross the access track by two kissing gates and bear right around the farm outbuildings to a kissing gate adjacent to the house. Turn left along the field edge now and look for a gate on the left, in the bottom corner of the field. A second gate immediately on the right leads through a small field to a quiet lane.

3. Turn right and follow the lane for about 300 yards to where a signed field path on the left leads back to Brynsiencyn. The path is well worn and well supplied with kissing gates.

Just before a farm, you will see the remains of a burial chamber in the field to your left. These remains date from a similar period to the more impressive Lligwy Burial Chamber (route 3 Moelfre) and like the restored monuments at Bryn Celli Ddu and Barclodiad y Grawres, would have been covered by a large mound of earth and stones. The stones that are visible today would originally have formed the 'chamber' where cremated remains were placed, often over long periods, before the chamber was finally sealed up. In the vast majority of cases, the mound has been eroded away leaving only the large stones of the inner chamber.

In the field beyond the farm, keep left and pass through two kissing gates to join a short track by houses. At the end of the track, turn right along the lane and return to Brynsiencyn. At the A4080 turn right again and return to point 1.

Mara Publications

Mara Publications publish a range of local walking books and have the following list to date:

A Walker's Guide to the Wirral Shore Way
ISBN 0 9522409 0 4. This book describes a linear walk of over 20 miles following Wirral's old coastline between Chester and Hoylake.

Circular Walks along the Sandstone Trail
ISBN 0 9522409 2 0. The Sandstone Trail is Cheshire's best known and most popular walking route. This book gives a complete route description along with 12 circular walks.

Walking in Wirral   ISBN 0 9522409 1 2.
A collection of 12 circular walks in Wirral.

Walking in the Clwydian Hills and the Vale of Llangollen
ISBN 0 9522409 3 9. A collection of circular walks in the beautiful hills and valleys of the Welsh borders.

Circular Walks along the Gritstone Trail and Mow Cop Trail
SBN 0 9522409 4 7. A route which follows Cheshire's eastern border along the edge of the Peak District. Following the same format as the Sandstone Trail book - a full route description for both trails is combined with 12 circular walks.

All the above publications are available from bookshops or by post direct from the publisher. Please check prices by telephone before ordering.

Forthcoming book:

Walking in Lleyn - exploring the coast and hills
ISBN 0 9522409 5 5. A collection of 15 walks on the coast and hills of the Lleyn Peninsula.